The Oath at Valley Forge. From a painting by Schmalze. Description on reverse of this leaf.

While Washington was reading the oath to his Staff Officers at Valley Forge he noted that Charles Lee had removed his hand from the Bible. Upon being asked why he did this Lee replied that he was not averse to renouncing his allegiance to the King of England but he had scruples in renouncing allegiance to the Prince of Wales. It is said that the other officers laughed and the administering of the Oath proceeded. It is this moment of hesitancy that the artist has depicted.

Some of the Earliest
Oaths of Allegiance

to the

United States of America

Nellie Protsman Waldenmaier, A.B.
*Member of the National Society Daughters of the American Revolution;
The National Genealogical Society;
Virginia Historical Society*

CLEARFIELD COMPANY

Originally published
1944

Reprinted for
Clearfield Company, Inc. by
Genealogical Publishing Co., Inc.
Baltimore, Maryland
1993, 1995

International Standard Book Number: 0-8063-4548-9

Made in the United States of America

PREFACE

IN preparing the material contained in this volume the editor has had in mind two objectives: first, the presentation of the data to be found in the oaths themselves; and, second, to present a brief outline of the historic background of the oaths.

The information found in the oaths themselves is of inestimable value to genealogists and to other historians. It is hoped that the time has passed when the genealogist was looked upon as merely a compiler of a limited range of vital statistics. The usefulness of the material in these oaths in genealogical research far exceeds the bare fact that a given individual "took and subscribed" the oath on a certain day. The existence of a man's name in this roster of patriots is indisputable evidence that he was a person trusted by the Continental Congress. The range of military leaders is all the way from the Commander in chief to express riders and "waggon" conductors; that of civil officials is equally comprehensive. The groupings of names is of obvious significance to the genealogist, especially in the case of identical surnames. The repetition of the oath by one man sometimes proves his advancement from one position to another of greater importance. Within the oaths themselves there is further evidence for a genealogist's interest which it is impossible for this editor to develope. For example there is the matter of handwriting and spelling. In the printed form of the prescribed oath the blanks for the deponent's name and office were filled in by a clerk; the final signature being an holograph one. This often furnishes an extremely interesting check on spelling and handwriting where there may be a question as to two men of the same name. These are only a few of the obvious clews to a man's identity and personality which are furnished by a study of the internal evidence of the oaths themselves.

As for the historic background of the Oath, that goes far back and down into the social, economic and political conditions that prevailed in 1778 and before. There were the aristocratic Tories who were afraid of losing their property; there were the Quakers and other conscientious objectors who were a constant thorn in the flesh of Washington and the Continental Congress; there were such men as Benedict Arnold and Charles Lee, both of whom did "take and subscribe" the required oath but who, even while doing so, must have had a mental reservation. All of these movements, and many more, are to be found elucidated in the Journals of the Continental Congress, the Writings of Washington, the Letters of the Members of the Continental Congress and a mass of other most fascinating source material.

To any one having even the most superficial knowledge of the pre-federal history of this country the mere reading of the list of the deponents of this oath presents a mind's-eye picture of personalities whose parade-like sequence furnishes a cavalcade of most notable significance. One begins with "George Washington, Commander in Chief of the Armies of the United States," whose oath was witnessed by Lord Stirling. Then follow the names of the Major Generals and the Brigadier Generals whose oaths, with the single exception of that of Benedict Arnold, were witnessed by Washington himself. Then come the next in rank on down the line each being witnessed by the superior officer. There are Senior Surgeons and Sugeon's Mates; there are quarter masters and deputy quarter masters; waggon masters and forage masters; there are express riders and artificers; there are a few individuals identified simply as "volunteers." In the civil list the pageant is no less noteworthy. There are the clerks in the offices of the Continental Congress. Later there are the secretaries (cabinet officers) who headed the executive departments. Finally, the territorial growth of the nation is heralded by the passing in review of such names as Arthur St. Clair, Governor of the Northwest Territory; Winthrop Sargent, Secretary "in and for" the Territory west of the River Ohio; and the three Judges who functioned under General (Governor) St. Clair.

The long list speaks for itself. I beg the reader to consider well the significance of each item of information accompanying the name of each signer, i.e., the date and place where the oath was taken; the witnessing official. There are instances where this information is not contained in the original oaths. In such instances the present editor has not presumed to supply it even though it might be easily available. In the course of several shiftings from one government department to another, and possibly in some other way, these oaths have become somewhat shuffled. However there is order in the apparent chaos of the arrangement as they are preserved and what order there is this editor has retained—as well as the disorder.

In the preparation of the material here presented the editor is deeply indebted to members of the staffs of both the Manuscript Division of the Library of Congress and of the National Archives. I wish especially to express my appreciation of the assistance of Miss Edna Vosper (since deceased) of the National Archives and of Miss Dorothy Vastine of the Library of Congress.

NELLIE P. WALDENMAIER

CONTENTS

	PAGE
PREFACE	iii
INTRODUCTION	1
OATHS OF ALLEGIANCE IN THE NATIONAL ARCHIVES	
Volume 165, Records of the War Department	20
Volume 166, Records of the War Department	33
Volume 167, Records of the War Department	42
Volume 168, Records of the War Department	51
OATHS OF ALLEGIANCE IN THE LIBRARY OF CONGRESS	64
ALPHABETICAL INDEX OF NAMES OF SIGNERS OF OATHS OF ALLEGIANCE	79

INTRODUCTION

"When, in the course of human events,"[1] it became necessary for those valiant fifty-six members of the Second Continental Congress to declare themselves the "representatives of the UNITED STATES OF AMERICA"; and did "solemnly publish and declare that these united colonies are and of right ought to be, free and independent states,"[1] they, by so declaring, changed the status of the North American Settlements from that of embryonic Colonies to that of full fledged, although somewhat tottery, UNITED STATES OF AMERICA.

The Revolution had begun before this, but had not passed the stage of being merely a revolt of rebellious colonies. On June 14, 1775, this same Continental Congress had passed a resolution providing for the raising of an "American continental Army"[2] and, on the following day Washington was unanimously chosen commander in chief of that Army.[2] The year intervening between these two momentous events (June, 1775 to July, 1776) had been one of great trial and often error. One of the most important developments of this trial period was the recognition of the necessity for the struggling Patriots to know who were their friends and supporters and who were not their friends and might be their enemies.

CIVIL WAR

In speaking of this period Lafayette said:[3] "Notwithstanding the independence of the new States there was then everywhere the evidence of civil war. The names Whig and Tory distinguished the Republicans and Royalists; the English army was still called the regular troops; in speaking of the king, the British sovereign was meant. Furious partisanship divided provinces, cities and families; brothers who were officers in the opposing armies met in the paternal households and sprang to arms to fight each other." * * *

"Each community included a large number whose sole object was to annoy the friends of liberty, to aid those of despotism. To these inveterate Tories there were added those whom fear, self interest or religion kept out of war. If the Presbyterians, children of Cromwell and Fairfax, hated royalty, the Anglicans, of whom they were a part, were even more divided. The Quakers hated bloodshed, but served

---

[1] Declaration of Independence.
[2] Albert Bushnell Hart, Formation of the Union, 1750–1829, p. 75.
[3] Memoires, correspondance et manuscrits du General Lafayette, publiee par Sa Famille, Bruxelles, 1837, p. 18.

George Washington. Commander in chief of the Armies of the United States of America

I do acknowledge the UNITED STATES of AMERICA, to be Free, Independent and Sovereign States, and declare that the people thereof owe no allegiance or obedience to George the Third, King of Great-Britain; and I renounce, refuse and abjure any allegiance or obedience to him; and I do *swear* —— that I will to the utmost of my power, support, maintain and defend the said United States, against the said King George the Third, his heirs and successors and his or their abettors, assistants and adherents, and will serve the said United States in the office of *Commander in chief as aforesaid* which I now hold, with fidelity, according to the best of my skill and understanding.

Sworn before me.
Camp at Valley Forge.
May 12th 1778.   G. Washington
Stirling Major gen'l

Oath of Washington. This was the prescribed form but there were variations as is seen in other forms illustrated.

INTRODUCTION 3

as guides to the royal troops; insurrections were not uncommon; near the outposts of the enemy farmers shot each other; stealing was encouraged. In traveling through the country the patriot leaders took great risks. They announced themselves to be in one house and then lodged in another. They barricaded themselves in and slept fully armed."

On the same subject John Adams said: "That there existed a general desire of independence of the Crown in any part of America before the Revolution, is as far from the truth as the Zenith is from the Nadir." [4] This being the state of public opinion we can well understand that, during this period of labor pains, there were developed all shades and degrees of Loyalty and Toryism.

Disaffection to the American Cause

The immediate result of the Declaration of Independence was to "oblige every American to take sides for or against the Revolution." [5] Congress recognized the fact that it was highly important to exclude from the public service all persons who could not be trusted to support the new government. With this end in view various committees were appointed from time to time to determine what was to be done about "persons disaffected to the American cause." These committees usually recommended that persons suspected of being so disaffected should be required to take some kind of an Oath giving assurance of their fidelity.

Oath of Fidelity in Office

As early as July 29, 1775, Congress had provided for an Oath of Fidelity in Office by the resolution, "That the paymaster general, commissary general, quarter master general, and every (sic) of their deputies, shall take an Oath truly and faithfully to discharge the duties of their respective stations." [6] Also, on June 18, 1776, there was passed the so-called Tory Act which provided for the fair trial of suspected Tories and ordered the printing of this resolution. It was printed in the Pennsylvania Gazette, June 19, 1776.

However, the Oath to render a true account of monies and goods belonging to the government was not a sufficient guaranty of allegiance, once the colonies had become the United States of America.

[4] Hart, p. 77.
[5] Ibid., p. 80.
[6] Journals of Congress, Vol. II, p. 223.

Oaths of Army Officers

On September 18, 1776, Congress "Resolved, That the Board of War be directed to prepare a resolution for enforcing and perfecting discipline in the army." [7] As a consequence of this resolution there was written into the Articles of War (Sept. 20, 1776) a provision requiring "every non-commissioned officer and soldier to take the following Oath: "I swear, or affirm, (as the case may be) to be true to the United States of America, and to serve them honestly and faithfully against all their enemies or opposers whatsoever, and to observe and obey the orders of the Continental Congress and the orders of the officers set over me by them." [8]

Evidently this was not entirely satisfactory to the Congress for a month later, on October 10, 1776, that body "Resolved, That a committee of three be appointed to prepare the form of an oath to be taken by the officers of the army and navy." The members of this committee were Mr. George Wythe, Mr. Thomas Stone, and Mr. Robert Treat Paine.[9] On October 21, 1776, the report of this committee was taken into consideration and it was agreed that all "officers in the service of the Continent" should subscribe the following Oath:

"I, ..., do acknowledge the Thirteen United States of America, namely, New Hampshire, Massachusetts Bay, Rhode Island, Connecticut, New York, New Jersey, Pennsylvania, Delaware, Maryland, Virginia, North Carolina, South Carolina and Georgia, to be free, independent and sovereign states, and declare that the people thereof owe no allegiance or obedience to George the third, king of Great Britain; and I renounce, refuse and abjure any allegiance or obedience to him; and I do swear, that I will, to the utmost of my power, support, maintain, and defend the said United States against the said George the third, and his heirs and successors, and his and their abettors, assistants and adherents; and will serve the said United States in the office of .... which I now hold, and in any other office which I may hereafter hold, by their appointment or under their authority, with fidelity and honor according to the best of my skill and understanding. So help me God." [10]

This form seems to be so comprehensive as to have called for no material change. However, there were numerous other forms used expecially for the purpose of assuring fidelity in office. For example:

"We, and each of us, do swear that we will deliver all the copies of the articles of confederation which we shall print, together with the copy sheet

[7] Ibid., Vol. V, p. 781.
[8] Ibid., Vol. V, p. 790.
[9] Ibid., Vol. VI, 861.
[10] Ibid., Vol. VI, 893–894.

INTRODUCTION 5

to the Secretary of Congress and that we will not disclose either directly or indirectly the contents of said confederation.

"Philadelphia, July 13, 1776. (signed)
"Sworn before me John Dunlap.
"John Gibson. D. C. Claypoole." [11]

Also this:

"Form of Oath of Office in the Secretary's Office of Congress, 22nd March, 1777. I, Belcher P. Smith, do swear well and faithfully to execute the Trust reposed in me in the Capacity of Clerk in the Secretary's Office of Congress, according to the best of my skill and Judgment; and to disclose no Matter the Knowledge of which I may acquire in Consequence of such my office which I may be directed to keep secret.

                                        (signed)
"Sworn before me Belcher P. Smith.[12]
"John Hancock, Pres't. June 30, 1777."

And so the effort to satisfactorily word an Oath that would meet all requirements went on for a year and a half. Then, on December 26, 1777, Congress "Resolved, That a committee of three be appointed to devise effectual means to prevent persons disaffected to the interest of the United States from being employed in any of the important offices thereof."

The members of this committee were Mr. Daniel Roberdeau, Mr. Abraham Clark and Mr. William Ellery.[13]

On January 21, 1778 the above committee recommended the adoption of the following Resolution:

"Resolved, That all commissioned officers in the Army and Navy of the United States, the Commissioners of the Navy boards; the Quarter Master General, Deputy Quarter Masters General; Commissaries of Forage, forage master; Commissaries of Stores, deputies and assistant quarter masters; the Commissary General and deputy Commissary generals of Purchase and Issues, and their deputies and assistant Commissaries; all Commissaries of other departments; all Officers of the Staff in the Army; the Treasurer, Auditor general, Deputy auditor general and all other auditors and Commissaries; the Post Master, Surveyor and Comptroller general of Post office, Postmasters and post riders; the Clothier General and his Deputies; the Director General, deputy directors and all Surgeons and Physicians of the Hospitals and Army; and all clerks in every public office and Department, who are already appointed, shall within one month after notice hereof, and all such as may hereafter be appointed and accept of their appointment, immediately thereupon, previous to acting therein, severally take and subscribe the following oath (or if one of the people called quakers, Affirmation)

[11] Mss. Oaths in Library of Congress Collection, p. I.
[12] Ibid., p. 4.
[13] Journals of Congress, Vol. IX, p. 1053.

filling up the blank with their name and office. "I, ..., do solemnly swear, or affirm, that I acknowledge the thirteen United States of America, namely, New Hampshire, Massachusetts Bay, Rhode Island and Providence Plantations, Connecticut, New York, New Jersey, Pennsylvania, Delaware, Maryland, Virginia, North Carolina, South Carolina and Georgia, to be free Sovereign and Independent States, and that the people thereof owe no Allegiance or obedience to George the third, King of Great Britain, and that neither the said king nor the Parliament of Great Britain nor any foreign Prince, Power or Potentate whatsoever ought to have any power, right, Authority or jurisdiction over the said United States or any of them or the Subjects thereof. And that I will to the utmost of my power support, maintain and defend the said United States against the said King George the third, his heirs, and successors, and his and their agents, abettors and assistants, and will faithfully serve the said United States in the office I now hold and in any other office which I may hereafter hold by their appointment or under their authority, according to the best of my skill and understanding. So help me God." [14]

The report of this committee also recommended that this oath be signed in duplicate and one copy be kept by the Deponent and the other copy, in the case of the Military Line, "be sent to the commander in chief and by him to the Secretary of Congress; in the case of the Navy these Oaths were to be sent to the Navy Board most convenient and by them to the Marine Committee. This report is in the handwriting of Abraham Clark. Congress ordered that it be "taken into consideration tomorrow." [15]

The Oath as Finally Worded

This "tomorrow" stretched out until February 3, 1778, when Congress considered this committee report and

"Resolved, That every officer who holds a commission or shall hereafter hold a commission or office from Congress, shall take and subscribe the following Oath or Affirmation:

"I, ..., do acknowledge the UNITED STATES OF AMERICA to be Free Independent and Sovereign States, and declare that the people thereof owe no allegiance or obedience to George the Third, King of Great Britain; and I renounce, refuse and abjure any allegiance or obedience to him; and I do swear (or affirm) that I will, to the utmost of my power, support, maintain and defend the said United States against the said King George the Third, his heirs and successors and his or their abettors, assistants and adherents, and will serve the said United States in the office of .... which I now hold, with fidelity, according to the best of my skill and understanding." [16]

[14] Ibid., Vol. X, pp. 68–70.
[15] Ibid., Vol. X, p. 73.
[16] Ibid., Vol. X, p. 114.

INTRODUCTION 7

When the vote on the adoption of this resolution was taken, all votes were in the affirmative except the two from Maryland. These were cast by Mr. Forbes and Mr. Henry. The members voting for the resolution were:[17]

New York..........Mr. Frost.
Massachusetts......Mr. Ellery.
Connecticut........Mr. Dyer.
New Jersey.........Mr. Witherspoon and Mr. Clark.
Pennsylvania.......Mr. Roberdeau, Mr. Clingan and Mr. J. B. Smith.
Delaware...........Mr. McKean.
Virginia............Mr. F. L. Lee.
North Carolina.....Mr. Penn.
South Carolina.....Mr. Laurens.
Georgia............Mr. Langworthy and Mr. Wood.

This resolution provided that this Oath was to be signed in duplicate and that

"Every officer shall deliver or transmit one of the certificates obtained to the commander in chief or the commander of the department, or to such as by general orders shall be appointed to receive the same; and the said commanding officers shall cause the certificates so received to be sent to the Secretary of Congress, and shall keep an exact list of the names of all officers whose certificates shall be received and forwarded, together with their several ranks and the time of their being qualified.

"That every officer of the Navy shall deliver or send one of the certificates by him obtained to the navy board most convenient who are required to transmit the same, and also a certificate of their own qualifications, to the Marine Committee, as soon as conveniently may be.

"That every other person employed in any civil department or office, as above mentioned, shall send or deliver one of the certificates by him obtained to the secretary of the state to which he belongs, or to such other person or persons as the governor or president of such State shall direct; and the governors or presidents of the several states are hereby requested to attend to this matter, and to cause the certificates, when received, to be transmitted to the secretary of Congress.

"That each deponent or affirmant shall retain and keep the other certificate by him obtained, as a voucher of his having complied with what is hereby enjoined him."[18]

Twenty days were allowed for present incumbents in office to take this Oath "after notice hereof."

[17] Ibid., Vol. X, p. 115.
[18] Ibid., Vol. X, p. 116.

And so, after a year and a half of congressional discussion, the wheels of the machinery were set turning for the other officers of the new nation, both civil and military, to follow the example of the fifty-six signers of the Declaration of Independence and so place themselves on record as being actively on the side of the UNITED STATES OF AMERICA. The wording of that Oath had been carefully worked out and, in its final form, it represented the composite efforts of several different committees and of Congress as a body. Washington called it an "Oath of Abjuration, Fidelity and Allegiance." It was all of that and there can be no doubt of the seriousness with which it was received by the officers who were called upon to sign it.

Administering the Oath

Within the twenty days of Grace allowed by the resolution many of the officers, both civil and military, who were stationed in York Town (York, Pa.) had taken both the Oath of Allegiance and the Oath of Fidelity in Office. The form of this latter oath was:

"I, ..., do swear that I will faithfully, truly and impartially execute the office of .... to which I have been appointed and render a true account, when required, of all monies by me received or expended and of all stores and other effects to me entrusted, which belong to the United States, and will in all respects, discharge the trust reposed in me with justice and integrity to the best of my skill and understanding." [19]

On the third of March following the passage of the resolution, that part of the Continental Army which was under the command of Major General William Heath, and was stationed at Boston,[20] began taking the prescribed Oath and continued from day to day, Sundays excepted.

At Fish Kill,[21] on the Hudson, those officers under Major General Alexander McDougall began, on May 7, 1778, and continued for a month to subscribe their names to those momentous bits of paper.

If the necessary printed forms were not at hand, substitute forms were written out in long hand. These written forms sometimes follow the wording of the printed form verbatim; sometimes they are a most interesting conglomeration of the various forms that had been proposed by different Congressional committees; sometimes they are entirely original compositions of either the deponent himself or of the officer administering the Oath. When we reverently read these clear,

---

[19] Writings of Washington, edited by John C. Fitzpatrick, Vol. II, p. 362.
[20] Oaths in Library of Congress.
[21] Ibid.

but often verbose, statements today, as we find them in the precious government documents, these variations from the norm afford a definitely human touch. One man added to his formal Oath, "So help me God,—Pray God keep me steadfast in what I have undertaken." [22] There was nothing perfunctory in the oath of a man who added that little prayer.

WASHINGTON AND THE OATH

Very soon after the passage of the resolution of February 3, 1778, Washington must have received formal notice thereof. Under date of February 14, 1778, he wrote a letter to the President of Congress in which he said, "The Oath which Congress have prescribed to be taken by the officers of the Army, I shall publish in General Orders and the mode how it is to be done with directions about the certificates." [23] However this action on the part of Washington was for some reason delayed. More than two months after the passage of the resolution Henry Laurens, President of Congress, wrote to Washington:

"April 27, 1778.[24]
* * * * * *
"I am directed by Congress to request Your Excellency will immediately require all officers Civil as well as Military in the Army, who are at present delinquent, to comply with the terms of an Act of Congress of the 3rd of Febry last by taking the Oath of Allegiance and Abjuration and that Your Excellency will be pleased to cause the necessary Certificates as speedily as possible to be returned and, if occasion shall be given, which is supposed to be scarcely possible, the name or Names of such persons as shall refuse. * * *

"The bearer hereof will deliver three Packets containing about 600 blanks which will hasten the business of Administering the Oaths. More shall be sent by the next messenger."

On May 1, 1778, Washington replied to this letter as follows: [25]

"Sir: I have had the honour to receive your dispatches of the 27th Inst. In compliance with the request of Congress I shall immediately call upon the Officers in the Army to take the Oath of Allegiance and Abjuration. This I should have done, as soon as the Resolution passed, had it not been for the state of the Army at the time, and that there were some strong reasons which made it expedient to defer the matter."

[22] Oaths in National Archives, Vol. 167, No. 29.
[23] Fitzpatrick, Vol. 10, p. 429.
[24] E. C. Burnett, Letters of Members of the Continental Congress, Vol. III, p. 190.
[25] Fitzpatrick, Vol. 10, p. 331.

Another week went by. Then, in General Orders, we find:

"Head Quarters, Valley Forge, Thirsday(sic), May 7, 1778. "The honorable Congress have been pleased by their resolution of the 3rd of February last to require of all Officers, as well civil as military, holding Commissions under them to take and subscribe the following Oath or Affirmation according to Circumstances of the Parties."

(Here follows the Oath as quoted above in the Resolution.) Then General Orders continue:

"In order to accomplish this very interesting and essential work as early as possible the following Officers are to administer the Oath and grant Certificates to the Officers of the Divisions, Brigades or Corps set against their names including the Staff. Major General Stirling to the Officers of Late Conway's Brigade; Major General Marquis De la Fayette to those of Woodford's and Scott's Brigade; Major General De Kalb to those of Glover's and Larned's Brigades; General McIntosh to those of his own Brigade; General Maxwell to those of his own Brigade; Brigadier General Knox to those of the Artillery in Camp and Officers of Military Stores; General Poor to those of his own Brigade; General Varnum to those of his own and General Huntington's Brigade; Brigadier General Patterson to those of his own Brigade; Brigadier General Wayne to those of the First and Second Pennsylvania Brigades; General Muhlenberg to those of his own and Weedon's Brigade. Printed Copies of the Oath will be immediately lodged in the hands of Major and Brigadier Generals to facilitate the business.

"The Generals administering the Oath are to take Duplicates of the same and to grant Certificates when it is made. In the beginning of the Oath the Name, Rank and Corps of the Party making it are to be inserted. The Duplicate of the Oath and Certificate is to be returned to Head Quarters by the Generals, who will also keep those respecting the Officers of each Regiment by themselves that an Arrangment of the whole may be made out with greater ease and accuracy.

"Major General Greene is to administer the Oath and grant the like Certificates to the Officers of his department. The Commissaries of Provisions both Issuing and Purchasing and to the Commissary of Forage and his Deputies; Besides which he is to administer to the said officers the following Oath and grant duplicate Certificates.[27] "

(Here follows the Oath of Fidelity in Office, see above.)

Evidently these General Orders did not bring immediate results for on May 11, 1778, Washington wrote to Lord Stirling:[28]

"My Lord: I have received your letter of yesterday's date. I had no particular person in view when I issued the order respecting the slow progress

---

[26] Orderly Book at Valley Forge, covering period from April 18 to July 21, 1778; in National Archives.
[27] Fitzpatrick, Vol. II, 360.
[28] Ibid., Vol. II, p. 374.

INTRODUCTION

of the Works, at the same time I acknowledge that I am exceedingly mortified at seeing, and beholding the delay of them, whether unavoidable, or not, I do not undertake to determine.

"Colos. Brearly and Barber inform me that the Officers of their Regiments are now ready to take the Oaths, and as there is some little boggle in this matter in other Corps I must beg your Lordship to administer them without delay as it will be a good example to others." [28]

Washington wrote from:

"Head Quarters, Valley Forge, Monday, May 11, 1778.

"The General Officers are requested to attend at Head Quarters tomorrow at eleven O'clock in the forenoon, that they may take the Oath appointed by Congress in their Resolution of the 3rd of February last which was published in General Orders of the 7th Inst." [29]

In spite of all this preparation and delay there must still have been some "boggle in the matter" as is shown by an exchange of letters between Washington and Lafayette. This "boggle" was undoubtedly a reverberation of that notorious effort to displace Washington as commander in chief and install General Gates in that position,—that discordant fiasco known as the Conway Cabal.

Lafayette to Washington:

"Valley Forge Camp, the 15th of May, 1778.

"My Dear General: Agreeable to Your Excellency's orders, I have taken the oath of the gentlemen officers in General Woodford's brigade, and their certificates have been sent to the adjutant-general's office. Give me leave, now, to present you some observations delivered to me by many officers of that brigade, who desire me to submit them to your perusal. I know, sir, (besides I am not of their opinion in the fact itself) that I should not accept for you the objections those gentlemen could have had as a body, to any order from congress; but I confess the desire of being agreeable to them, of giving them any mark of friendship and affection which is in my power, and acknowledging the kind sentiments they honor me with, have been by first and dearest consideration. Besides that, be pleased to consider that they began by obeying orders, and want only to let their loved general know which were the reasons of their being rather reluctant (as far as reluctance may comply with their duty and honor) to an oath, the meaning and spirit of which, I believe, was misunderstood by them. I may add, sir, with perfect conviction, that there is not one among them but would be thrice happy were occasion offered them of distinguishing yet by new exertions their love of their country, their zeal for their duty as officers, their consideration for the civil power, and their love for your excellency.

"with greatest respect and most tender affection,—I have the honor &c:"

[29] Ibid., Vol. II, p. 375.
[30] Memoires, Lafayette, Vol. I, p. 170.

To which Letter Washington replied:[31]

"Head Quarters, Valley Forge, May 17, 1778.
"Dear Sir: I received yesterday your favor of the 15th Inst. inclosing a paper subscribed by Sundry Officers of General Woodford's brigade, setting forth their reasons for not taking the Oath of Abjuration, Allegiance and Office, and thank you for the cautious delicacy used in communicating the matter to me.

"As every Oath should be a free act of the Mind founded on the conviction of the party, of its propriety, I would not wish, in any instance that there should be the least degree of compulsion exercised; or to interpose my opinion in order to induce any to make it, of whom it is required. The Gentlemen therefore, who signed the paper will use their own discretion in the matter, and swear or not swear, as their conscience and feelings dictate.

"At the same time, I cannot but consider it as a circumstance of some singularity, that the scruples against the Oath should be peculiar to the Officers of one Brigade, and so very extensive. The Oath in itself is not New. It is substantially the same with that required in all Governments, and, therefore, does not imply any indignity; And it is perfectly consistent with the professions, Actions, and implied engagements of every Officer.

"The objections, founded on the supposed unsettled rank of the Officers, is of no validity (rank being only mentioned as a further designation of the party swearing); Nor can it be seriously thought, that the Oath is either intended, or can prevent their being promoted, or their resignations.

"The fourth objection stated by the Gentlemen, serves as a key to their scruples, and I would willingly persuade myself, that their own reflections will point out to them the impropriety of the whole proceeding, and suffer them to be betrayed in future into a similar conduct. I regard them all, and cannot but regret that they were engaged in the measure. I am certain they will regret it themselves; (Sure I am they ought)."

Jared Sparks seems to be the only authority for any evidence, other than the above letters, as to the reasons set forth by the officers who objected to taking the Oath. Sparks states that there were twenty-six officers of General Woodford's brigade who signed the "paper" to which Washington referred. The fourth reason set forth by them Sparks quotes as being:[32]

"4. The taking of the oath, while the present establishment continues, most of the subscribers are of opinion, would lay them under a pointed restraint in endeavoring to procure a change, which the whole army have long, not only ardently wished for, but conceived absolutely necessary for its preservation; a change, that would put them on an honorable and advantageous footing."

[31] Fitzpatrick, Vol. II, p. 410.
[32] Jared Sparks, Writings of Washington, 1837, Vol. V, pp. 267n–368.

Notwithstanding the objections of these twenty-six officers, we have Lafayette's word that they did take the Oath as prescribed. And thus the last bogie was exorcised by Washington's perfect understanding and tactful handling of a delicate situation.

THE OATHS TODAY

There remain to us, after more than a century and a half, these yellowed bits of paper, mute witnesses to the intrepid determination of the leaders of our forefathers in following Washington's Star of Faith in the destiny of this nation.
Not all of the Oaths that were sworn and subscribed are in existence. There must have been many that it has been impossible for this editor to locate. Those which have been located, and from which the accompanying material is drawn, are in two Government depositories. The largest of these collections is in the War Department Records in The National Archives. Here are four volumes which measure $14\frac{1}{2}$ by $17\frac{1}{2}$ inches; these are scrap books in which are mounted twelve hundred and eighteen of the original Oaths. Each oath, if it is on the printed form, is $6\frac{1}{2}$ by $4\frac{1}{4}$ inches. As has been said, there are many variations. The first of these volumes (numbered 165 in the War Department files) is a rather ornate tome, having gilt edges and a printed title page, which reads:

"Oaths of Allegiance to the United States by Officers at Valley Forge, 1777–1778.
"'Resolved, That every officer who holds, or shall hereafter hold, a commission or office from Congress, shall subscribe the above declaration, and take the foregoing Oath.'
"(In Congress Monday, Oct. 21, 1775.)"

All things considered that is a most astonishing title page. In the first place the Oaths contained in this volume were not all taken at Valley Forge; nor are they all of the oaths that were taken by the officers at Valley Forge. Secondly, none of the oaths therein contained was taken as early as 1777. And thirdly, the Resolution quoted is not the one which provided for the taking of this particular Oath. This Oath was provided for by the Resolution of February 3, 1778. (See Washington's General Orders.) However, there is the title page and there are the oaths. The other three volumes of this collection are without title page or decoration of any kind. Altogether these four volumes contain twelve hundred and eighteen Oaths.

In the Manuscript Division of the Library of Congress there is the other collection of these historic documents. This collection is similar to that in the National Archives as to external form. It has added interest in that the deponents are to a greater extent holders of civil posts. There are three scrap books in this collection and they contain three hundred and ninety-four Oaths.

Also, in the Library of Congress there is an old ledger labeled: "Alphabetical Index of Signers of the Oath of Allegiance." This book is not dated. The names contained in this Index are all to be found in the Library of Congress collection, with three exceptions. However there are many Oaths in this collection which are not listed in this Index. The three who are in the Index and whose Oaths have not been located are: William Churchill Huston (Houston), Thomas Franklin, Jr., and John Wharton. Whether these men signed the Oath and their certificates were lost or whether they refused to sign or did not sign for some unknown reason, I have no way of knowing.

Besides these collected Oaths there is one single Oath that is especially interesting, not only in itself, but because of its history. It will be noted that when the Continental Congress directed the taking of this Oath, they also directed that it was to be signed in duplicate. The deponent was to keep one copy as evidence of his compliance with the requirement of Congress. It would seem that this feature of the Resolution was variously interpreted. Among the Oaths as they exist there are some exact duplicates showing that some witnessing officers did not distinguish between an Oath and a Certificate. Also that the deponent did not take his own copy. In other cases there are certificates and no Oaths. In volume 166 of the National Archives collection, beginning with number 292, there are some twenty certificates all signed by Thomas Conway, which read:

"I do hereby certify that Ezekiel Brown, Surgeon of the Regiment of Foot Commanded by Ichabod Alden, Esq., did take the Oath of Allegiance to the United States of America, as prescribed by a Resolve of Congress, bearing date the 3rd of February, 1778. In Witness whereof I have signed and delivered the present Certificate. Albany, May 11, 1778.
(signed) Thomas Conway."

(Names, of course, vary but the above is an example.)

There must have been thousands of these Oaths and Certificates distributed throughout the thirteen States. One of these has come back to the Government records through the Revolutionary Pension application of the widow of the deponent, one Captain Samuel Lapsley of Colonel Nathaniel Gist's Regiment of Virginia. Captain Lapsley moved to Kentucky. There he died. His widow married a man named Lyle. He died. Then the widow applied for a pension and filed Captain Lapsley's Oath of Allegiance as evidence of his service. This Oath was witnessed by Lafayette and is dated May 17, 1778. It is the only Oath I have seen which was witnessed by Lafayette although he must have witnessed many.

Altogether there are one thousand six hundred and thirteen of these oaths preserved in the collections herein mentioned. Where are the thousands of others which did at one time exist? Perhaps the answer to this question is to be found in the history of the several very destructive fires that have taken their toll of government records. Perhaps they are still tucked away among papers not yet cataloged. It is to be hoped the latter is the case in regard to the copies kept for record. Of those retained by the deponents, surely that of Samuel Lapsley is not the only one in existence. Let us hope that others will be produced from their hiding places.

Meantime let us be thankful for these which have been so carefully preserved. They are unequivocal endorsement of the action of the fifty-six men who signed the Declaration of Independence and for that, if for no other reason, they are deserving of our most respectful attention.

N. P. W.

OATHS OF ALLEGIANCE

in the

RECORDS OF THE WAR DEPARTMENT

in

THE NATIONAL ARCHIVES

Note: The following Oaths are mounted in four Volumes. The Oaths are numbered, but t volumes are not paged. The numbering is not consecutive throughout. The numbers in t left hand side of the following list are the numbers of the oaths as they appear in these volum Following are the abbreviations used for the names of witnesses and places.

ABBREVIATIONS USED FOR OATHS IN NATIONAL ARCHIVES

A.—Albany
AP.—Artillery Park. (At Valley Forge)
B.—Bethlehem
C.—Conyingham
C.P.—C. Pulaski
DeS.—de Steuben
G.—Nathanael Green
G.W.—George Washington
Gph.—"At the Gulph" (Valley Forge)
H.—Huntington
Hld.—Highland
J.S.—John Stark
K.—Knox
K.F.—Camp at King's Ferry
L.—Benjamin Lincoln
M.—Peter Muhlenberg
McI.—Lachlan McIntosh

M.J.—Mount Joy (Valley Forge)
Mt.Pleas.—Mount Pleasant
N.B.—New Brunswick
N.W.—New Windsor
P.—Patterson
R.—Radnor
Rdg.—Reading
S.—Stirling
St.C.—Arthur St. Clair
T.—Trenton
T.C.—Thomas Conway
T.M.—Thomas Mifflin
V.—J. N. Varnum
VF.—Valley Forge
W.—Anthony Wayne
W.P.—White Plains

I *the Marquis de la fayette Major General in the Continental army* do acknowledge the UNITED STATES of AMERICA to be Free, Independent and Sovereign States, and declare that the people thereof owe no allegiance or obedience to George the Third, King of Great-Britain; and I renounce, refuse and abjure any allegiance or obedience to him; and I do *Swear* that I will, to the utmost of my power, support, maintain and defend the said United States against the said King George the Third, his heirs and successors, and his or their abettors, assistants and adherents, and will serve the said United States in the office of *Major General* which I now hold, with fidelity, according to the best of my skill and understanding.

Sworn before me this ___ the day ___ 1778
G. Washington

The Mis de Lafayette

Oath of Marquis de Lafayette.

Volume 165

RECORDS OF THE WAR DEPARTMENT

IN

THE NATIONAL ARCHIVES

Number	Deponent Office	Where taken	Date	Witness

1. George Washington, Commander in chief of the Armies of the United States of America...........................VF..........5-12-1778..S.
2. Charles Lee, Major General.............———.......6- 9-1778..G.W.
3. Nathanael Greene, Quarter Master General.............................———.......5-23-1778..G.W.
4. Nathanael Greene, Major General.......———.......5-23-1778..G.W.
5. Benedict Arnold, Major General.........AP at VF.....5-30-1778..K.
6. William Alexander, Earl of Stirling, Major General...........................VF......... 5-12-1778..G.W.
7. Arthur St. Clair, Major General ....VF..........5-12-1778..G.W.
8. Benjamin Lincoln, Major General.......———.......8-24-1778..G.W.
9. Marquis De Lafayette, Major General...———.......6- 9-1778..G.W.
10. John, Baron de Kalb, Major General.....VF..........5-12-1778..G.W.
11. Lachlan McIntosh, Brigadier General....VF..........5-12-1778..G.W.
12. De Steuben, Major General & Inspector General............................VF..........5-12-1778..G.W.
13. William Maxwell, Brigadier General.....VF..........5-22-1778..G.W.
14. William Smallwood, Brigadier General...———.......6- 9-1778..G.W.
15. Enoch Poor, Brigadier General..........VF..........5-12-1778..G.W.
16. James Mitchell Varnum,* Brigadier General............................VF..........5-12-1778..G.W.
17. John Patterson, Brigadier General.......VF..........5-12-1778..G.W.
18. Anthony Wayne, Brigadier General......VF..........5-12-1778..G.W.
19. William Woodford, Brigadier General....———.......6- 9-1778..G.W.
20. Peter Muhlenberg, Brigadier General....Camp........5-12-1778..G.W.
21. Charles Scott, Brigadier General.........Camp........6- 9-1778..G.W.
22. Louis the Chevalier du Portail, Brigadier General............................VF..........5-12-1778..G.W.
23. Robert H. Harrison, Lieutenant Colonel & Secretary to his Excellency, the Commander in Chief......................VF..........5-12-1778..S.
24. Tench Tilghman, Assistant Secretary to his Excellency the Commander in Chief ———.......5-12-1778..S.

* Affirmation.

Number	Deponent Office	Where taken	Date	Witness

25. Alexander Hamilton, Lieutenant Colonel & Aid-de-Camp to his Excellency, the Commander in Chief................VF..........5-12-1778..S.
26. Richard K. Meade, Lieutenant Colonel & Aid-de-Camp to his Excellency, the Commander in Chief................VF..........5-12-1778..S.
27. James McHenry, a Secretary to his Excellency, General Washington.........VF..........6- 9-1778..G.
28. John Laurens, Lieutenant Colonel & Aid-de-Camp to his Excellency, the Commander in Chief.....................VF..........5-12-1778..S.
29. Matthew Clarkson, Aid-de-Camp.......AP..........5—-1778..K.
30. David S. Franks, Aid-de-Camp.........AP..........5-30-1778..K.
31. Alexander Scammell, Colonel and Adjutant General......................VF..........5-12-1778..S.
32. Caleb Gibbs, Captain of his Excellency General Washington's Guards.........VF..........5-12-1778..S.
33. Henry P. Livingston, Lieutenant in his Excellency General Washington's Guards.VF..........5-12-1778..S.
34. William Colfax, Lieutenant in his Excellency General Washington's Guards....VF..........5-12-1778..S.
35. Benjamin Grymes, Lieutenant in his Excellency General Washington's Guards.VF..........5-12-1778..S.
36. James Craik, Assistant Director General in the Army of the United States......VF..........5-12-1778..S.
37. James Craik, Assistant Director General in the Army of the United States......VF..........5-12-1778..S.
38. Enoch Welsh, Ensign................B............3- 2-1778..K.
39. William Palfrey, Paymaster General.....Camp........2-28-1778..—
39½. Certificate from Stirling that No. 39 is true
40. Nathan Rice, Aid-de-Camp to Major General Lincoln......................———.......9- 1-1778..L.
41. Hodijah Baylies, Aid-de-Camp to Major General Lincoln......................———.......9—-1778..L.
42. Benjamin Walker, Captain & Aid-de-Camp............................VF..........5-22-1778..DeS.
43. John Ternant, Inspector of the Army....VF..........5-23-1778..DeS.
44. Peter Stephen Du Ponceau, Captain & Secretary.........................VF..........5-22-1778..DeS.
45. John Lawrence, Judge Advocate General in the Army of the United States of America..........................———.......6- 3-1778..M.

OATHS OF ALLEGIANCE

Number	Deponent	Office	Where taken	Date	Witness

46. John Brown Cutting, Apothecary General, Middle Department................ ———......5-30-1778..—
47. Thomas Tillotson, Physician and Surgeon.Pott's Grove..6- 6-1778..St.C.
48. Augustus Francis Des-Epiners, Major & Aid-de-Camp.....................VF.........5-22-1778..DeS.
49. Jacob Ehrenzeller, Jr., Surgeon General..Gph........7——1778..K.
50. Thomas Edwards, Adjutant............Gph........6-10-1778..K.
51. James Weems, Surgeon's Mate.........Gph........6-10-1778..K.
52. James Carew, Adjutant................Gph........6-10-1778..K.
53. William Barber, Ensign...............Gph........6-10-1778..K.
54. Nathaniel Thacher, Ensign............Gph........6-10-1778..K.
55. Edward Phelon, Ensign...............Gph........6-10-1778..K.
56. James Otis, Ensign...................Gph........6-10-1778..K.
57. John Smith, Ensign...................———......6-10-1778..K.
58. Peter Castaing, Second Lieutenant......Gph........6-10-1778..K.
59. Thomas Lamb, Lieutenant.............Gph........6-10-1778..K.
60. Charles Selden, Lieutenant............Gph........6-10-1778..K.
61. Samuel Rogers, Lieutenant............Gph........6-10-1778..K.
62. William Davis, Lieutenant.............Gph........6-10-1778..K.
63. Richard Walker, Lieutenant...........Gph........6-10-1778..K.
64. John Hobby, Lieutenant...............Gph........6-10-1778..K.
65. William Leverett, Lieutenant..........Gph........6-10-1778..K.
66. John Jackson, Lieutenant.............Gph........6-10-1778..K.
67. David Van Horne, Captain............Gph........6-10-1778..K.
68. Lemuel Trescott, Captain.............Gph........6-10-1778..K.
69. Thomas Turner, Lieutenant...........Gph........6-10-1778..K.
70. James Jones, Captain.................Gph........6-10-1778..K.
71. Gawen Brown, Captain...............Gph........6-10-1778..K.
72. Peter Dolliver, Captain................AP.........6-14-1778..K.
73. Nathaniel Jarvis, Captain.............Gph........6-10-1778..K.
74. Thomas Cartwright, Captain..........Gph........6-10-1778..K.
75. William North,* Captain..............Gph........6-10-1778..K.
76. John S. Tyler, Major..................Gph........6-10-1778..K.
77. William Hawks, Lieutenant...........AP.........6-14-1778..K.
78. William S. Smith, Lieutenant Colonel....———......6-10-1778..K.
79. Samuel H. Sullivan, Deputy Quarter Master General......................———......3-10-1778..C.P.
80. Lewis Nicola, Colonel of Regiment of Invalides...............................T............3- 7-1778..C.P.
81. James Paxton, Commissary...........T............3-10-1778..C.P.
82. William Henderson, Paymaster........———......2- 3-1778..C.P.

* "Affirm and swear."

RECORDS OF THE WAR DEPARTMENT—VOL. 165 23

| Number | Deponent Office | Where taken | Date | Witness |

83. John Cochran, Physician and Surgeon General to the Army of the United States................................VF..........5-10-1778..S.
84. George Draper, Second Surgeon.........VF..........5-20-1778..S.
85. William Bradford, Deputy Muster Master.VF..........5-20-1778..S.
86. Joseph Ward, Commissary General of Musters.............................VF..........5-20-1778..S.
87. William Barber, Aid-de-Camp to Major General Lord Stirling................VF..........5-16-1778..S.
88. James Monroe, Aid-de-Camp to Major General Lord Stirling................VF..........5-16-1778..S.
89. Isaac Budd, Aid-de-Camp to Major General Lord Stirling....................VF..........5-16-1778..S.
90. Conrad Latour, Second Lieutenant......VF..........5-21-1778..S.
91. Lawrence Myers (Mayers), First Lieutenant..............................VF..........5-21-1778..S.
92. Christian Maneke (Minka), First Lieutenant..............................VF..........5-21-1778..S.
93. Antoin Selm (Anthony Selim), Captain...VF..........5-21-1778..S.
94. John Stagg, Brigade Major..............VF..........5-29-1778..S.
95. John Brown Cutting, Apothecary General, Middle Department....................———.......5-29-1778..G.
96. Charles Pettit, Assistant Quarter Master General.............................———........3-23-1778..G.
97. Clement Biddle, Commissary General of Forage..............................———.......5-22-1778..G.
98. John Cox, Assistant Quarter Master General.............................———.......5-23-1778..G.
99. Robert Forsythe, Deputy Quarter Master General.............................———.....11-12-1778..G.
100. Clement Biddle, Commissary General of Forage..............................———.......5-22-1778..G.
101. Charles Porterfield, Quarter Master......———.......5-27-1778..G.
102. Archibald Steel, Deputy Quarter Master General.............................———.......5-22-1778..G.
103. Robert Forsythe, Deputy Quarter Master General.............................———.....10-19-1778..G.
104. Reuben Marsh, Waggon Conductor......———.......5-29-1778..G.
105. Daniel Kemper, Assistant Clothier General.............................———.......6-13-1778..G.
105½. Daniel Kemper, Assistant Clothier General.............................———.......6-13-1778..G.

24   OATHS OF ALLEGIANCE

Number   Deponent   Office   Where taken   Date   Witness
106. James Hamilton, Assistant Commissary
     of Issues .... NW .... 6-15-1778..G.
106½. James Hamilton, Assistant Commissary
     of Issues .... NW .... 6-15-1778..G.
107. John Corvell, Junior Surgeon to General
     Hospital ....,———...... 6- 3-1778..G.
108. Michael Harvey, Assistant Commissary
     of Issues .... Rdg .... 6-15-1778..G.
109. Michael Harvey, Assistant Commissary of
     Issues .... Rdg .... 6-15-1778..G.
110. John Nitche, Commissary in General Hos-
     pital ....———...... 6- 4-1778..G.
111. Joseph Hinderson, Waggon Conductor ...———...... 5-29-1778..G.
112. Aaron Matthews, Waggon Conductor ....———...... 5-29-1778..G.
113. Charles Connor, Waggon Conductor .....———...... 5-29-1778..G.
114. John J. Skidmore, Division Wagon Master.———...... 5-30-1778..G.
115. John White, Surgeon's Mate ....———...... 6- 2-1778..G.
116. Henry Crow, Assistant Apothecary,
     Middle Department ....———...... 6- 2-1778..G.
117. James Whitehead, Assistant to Commis-
     sary General of Forage ....———...... 5-31-1778..G.
118. William Marshall, Surgeon's Mate ......———...... 6- 2-1778..G.
119. William Armstrong, Assistant Commissary
     of Purchases ....———...... 6- 2-1778..G.
120. Samuel Morris, Commissary General of
     Hospitals .... "at Bake
                                           House, VF". 5-26-1778..G.
121. Nathan Wilkinson, Deputy Quarter Mas-
     ter General ....———...... 5-23-1778..G.
122. George W. Campbell, Second Surgeon ....———...... 5-26-1778..G.
123. John Shute,* Deputy Quarter Master
     General ....———...... 5-26-1778..G.
124. Marinus Willett, Surgeon's Mate ....———...... 5-26-1778..G.
125. Abel Morgan, Surgeon, "from Pa." ......———...... 5-26-1778..G.
126. John Mitchell, "of Phila. Co.," Deputy
     Quarter Master General ....———...... 5-26-1778..G.
127. Ebenezer Crosby, Second Surgeon ......———...... 5-26-1778..G.
128. Frederick Otto, Junior Surgeon ....·———...... 5-25-1778..G.
129. James Hutchinson, Senior Surgeon .....———...... 5-23-1778..G.
130. Charles Porterfield, Captain ....———...... 5-27-1778..G.
131. Adam Gilchrist, Assistant to Commissary
     General of Forage ....———...... 5-28-1778..G.

     * Affirmation.

RECORDS OF THE WAR DEPARTMENT—VOL. 165 25

Number	Deponent Office	Where taken	Date	Witness
132.	James Calhoun, Quarter Master General†.	—	5-22-1778	G.
133.	Joshua King, Forage Master	—	5-28-1778	G.
134.	Dudley L. Chase, Brigade Quarter Master.	—	5-28-1778	G.
135.	Charles Whittelsey, Brigade Quarter Master	—	5-28-1778	G.
136.	Charles Pettit, Assistant Quarter Master General	—	3-23-1778	G.
137.	John Cox, Assistant Quarter Master General	—	3-23-1778	G.
138.	Elijah Janes, Assistant Commissary of Issues	—	5-28-1778	G.
139.	George A. Baker, Assistant Commissary of Issues	—	5-28-1778	G.
140.	James Calhoun, Deputy Quarter Master General	—	5-22-1778	G.
141.	Paul Percival, Assistant Commissary of Issues	—	5-28-1778	G.
142.	Patrick Hackett, Assistant Commissary of Issues	"at Bake House, VF"	5-28-1778	G.
143.	Bernard Sweeny, Assistant Commissary of Issues	—	5-28-1778	G.
144.	Thomas Wiley, Assistant Commissary of Issues	—	5-28-1778	G.
145.	John Calhoun, Assistant Commissary of Purchases	—	5-28-1778	G.
146.	John Alexander Sapel, Surgeon's Mate..	—	5-29-1778	G.
147.	Matthias Sadler, Captain of Artificers....	—	5-29-1778	G.
148.	John Scott, Surgeon's Mate	—	5-29-1778	G.
149.	Thomas Alexander, Brigade Quarter Master	—	5-29-1778	G.
150.	Gustavus Risberg, Assistant Quarter Master of Issues	—	5-28-1778	G.
151.	Robert Baugh, Assistant Commissary of Issues	—	5-28-1778	G.
152.	David McKnight, Receiver of Cattle.....	—	5-28-1778	G.
153.	Benjamin Ballard, Assistant Commissary of Issues	—	5-28-1778	G.
154.	Michael Farley, Assistant Commissary of Issues	—	5-28-1778	G.
155.	Charles Lyon, Jr., Assistant Commissary of Issues	—	5-28-1778	G.

† From Maryland.

Number	Deponent Office	Where taken	Date	Witness
156.	George Morton, Assistant Commissary of Issues	—	5-28-1778	G.
157.	Simon Philips, Assistant Commissary of Issues	—	5-28-1778	G.
158.	John Cheesborough, from N. C., Assistant Commissary of Issues	—	5-28-1778	G.
159.	James Gamble, from Pa., Assistant Commissary of Issues	—	5-28-1778	G.
160.	Edward Lewis, Assistant Commissary of of Issues	—	5-28-1778	G.
161.	Alexander McCaraher, Commissary of the General Hospital Middle Department	—	5-30-1778	G.
162.	Alexander McCarkey, Deputy Commissary General of Forage	—	5-31-1778	G.
163.	Thomas Durie, Assistant to the Commissary General of Forage	—	5-31-1778	G.
164.	James Whitehead, Assistant to the Commissary General of Forage	—	5-31-1778	G.
165.	Janes Smith, Clerk to the Flying Hospital	—	5-31-1778	G.
166.	John Pool, Forage Master	—	5-31-1778	G.
167.	James Allen,[1] Brigade Quarter Master	—	5-27-1778	G.
168.	Minnie Voorhies, Commissary to the Flying Hospital of the Middle Department	—	5-27-1778	G.
169.	John Campbell, Assistant Commissary to the Flying Hospital, Middle, Department	—	5-27-1778	G.
170.	Lawrence Trant, Brigade Quarter Master	—	5-28-1778	G.
171.	John Flynn,[2] Forage Master	—	5-28-1778	G.
172.	Thomas Jones, Deputy Commissary of Issues of the Middle Department	—	5-28-1778	G.
173.	Thomas Ramsay,[2] Assistant Commissary of Issues	—	5-28-1778	G.
174.	John Kean, Assistant Commissary of Issues	—	5-28-1778	G.
175.	John Mitchell, Philadelphia County, Deputy Quarter Master General	—	5-26-1778	G.
176.	James Darrah, Assistant Commissary of Issues	—	5-26-1778	G.
177.	John B. Rodgers, Surgeon's Mate	—	5-29-1778	G.
178.	Gilbert Tennent, Surgeon's Mate	—	5-29-1778	G.

[1] Affirmation.
[2] From Pennsylvania.

Number	Deponent Office	Where taken	Date	Witness
179.	Timothy Whiting, Brigade Quarter Master		5-30-1778	G.
180.	Barnabas Binney, Senior Surgeon		5-30-1778	G.
181.	David Phillips, Commissary of the General Hospital of the Middle Department		5-30-1778	G.
182.	James Fallon, Senior Surgeon of the General Hospital of the Middle Department		5-30-1778	G.
183.	William W. Smith, Second Surgeon		5-28-1778	G.
184.	Ebenezer Clark, Assistant Commissary of Issues		5-28-1778	G.
185.	George Burroughs, Assistant Commissary of Issues		5-28-1778	G.
186.	Abishai Thomas,* Deputy Quarter Master General		5-22-1778	G.
187.	John Lillie, Brigade Quarter Master General		5-25-1778	G.
188.	Bodo Otto, Senior Surgeon		5-25-1778	G.
189.	Samuel Kennedy, Senior Surgeon		5-26-1778	G.
190.	Goodwin Wilson, Second Surgeon		5-26-1778	G.
191.	Peter Hartman, Waggon Master		5-30-1778	G.
192.	Thomas Marshall, Second Surgeon		5-30-1778	G.
193.	William Armstrong, Assistant Commissary of Purchases		6- 2-1778	G.
194.	William Evans, Assistant Commissary of Purchases		6- 2-1778	G.
195.	John Ingram, Sub Conductor of Waggons		5-29-1778	G.
196.	James Yule, Deputy Waggon Master General		5-29-1778	G.
197.	James McCashlin, Sub Conductor of Waggons		5-29-1778	G.
198.	Stephen Eldridge, Sub Conductor of Waggons		5-29-1778	G.
199.	Aaron Matthews, Waggon Conductor		5-29-1778	G.
200.	James Ranney (Rooney), Waggon Conductor			G.
201.	George Buyers, Sub Conductor of Waggons		5-29-1778	G.
202.	William Gray, Waggon Conductor		5-29-1778	G.
203.	Jacob Grace, Sub Conductor of Waggons		5-30-1778	G.
204.	Josiah Kittera, Waggon Conductor		5-30-1778	G.
205.	Hugh McClaran, Waggon Conductor		5-30-1778	G.

* From North Carolina.

28   OATHS OF ALLEGIANCE

| Number | Deponent Office | Where taken | Date | Witness |

206. Henry Gordon, Waggon Conductor......———.......5-29-1778..G.
207. Robert Riddle, Waggon Conductor......———.......5-29-1778..G.
208. David Philips, Commissary of the General
     Hospital of the Middle Department....———.......5-30-1778..G.
209. Abraham Rand, Sub Conductor of
     Waggons............................———.......5-30-1778..G.
209½. Thomas Durie, Assistant Commissary of
     Forage.............................———.......5-31-1778..G.
209¾. Charles Connor, Waggon Conductor....———.......5-29-1778..G.
210. Alexander McCaskey, Deputy Commis-
     sary General of Forage...............———.......5-31-1778..G.
211. Alexander McCaraher, Commissary of the
     General Hospital of the Middle Depart-
     ment..............................———.......5-30-1778..G.
212. Peter Hartman, Waggon Master.........———.......5-30-1778..G.
213. Timothy Whiting, Quarter Master......———.......—————..G.
214. James Fallon, Senior Surgeon..........———.......5-30-1778..G.
215. Charles Lyon, Jr., Assistant Commissary
     of Issues...........................———.......5-28-1778..G.
216. James Darrah, Assistant Commissary of
     Issues..............................———.......5-28-1778..G.
217. Simon Phillips, Assistant Commissary of
     Issues..............................———.......5-28-1778..G.
218. George Morton, Assistant Commissary
     of Issues...........................———.......5-28-1778..G.
219. John Cheesborough,[1] Assistant Commis-
     sary of Issues......................———.......5-28-1778..G.
220. Thomas Jones, Deputy Commissary Gen-
     eral of Issues......................———.......5-28-1778..G.
221. Thomas Ramsay,[2] Assistant Commissary
     of Issues...........................———.......5-28-1778..G.
222. Gustavus Risberg, Assistant Commissary
     of Issues...........................———.......5-28-1778..G.
223. John Flynn, Forage Master............———.......5-28-1778..G.
224. John Campbell, Assistant Commissary of
     the Flying Hospital..................———.......5-27-1778..G.
225. Lawrence Trant, Brigade Quarter Master.———.......5-28-1778..G.
226. James Allen,[3] Brigade Quarter Master....———.......5-27-1778..G.
227. Minnie Voorhies, Commissary of the Fly-
     ing Hospital........................———.......5-27-1778..G.

[1] From North Carolina.
[2] From Pennsylvania.
[3] Affirmation.

RECORDS OF THE WAR DEPARTMENT—VOL. 165

Number	Deponent Office	Where taken	Date	Witness
228.	John Kean, Assistant Commissary of Issues............................	————	5-28-1778	G.
229.	James Smith, Clerk in the Flying Hospital.————		5-31-1778	G.
230.	John Pool, Forage Master............... ————		5-31-1778	G.
231.	Matthias Sadler, Captain of Artificers.... ————		5-29-1778	G.
232.	Archibald Steel, Deputy Quarter Master General............................ ————		5-22-1778	G.
233.	John Chaloner, Assistant Commissary of Purchases........................... ————		5-29-1778	G.
234.	John Alexander Sapel, Surgeon's Mate... ————		5-29-1778	G.
235.	Thomas Alexander,[1] Brigade Quarter Master............................ ————		5-29-1778	G.
236.	John Scott, Surgeon's Mate............ ————		5-29-1778	G.
237.	David McKnight, Receiver of Cattle..... ————		5-28-1778	G.
238.	Elijah Janes, Assistant Commissary of Issues............................ ————		5-28-1778	G.
239.	Patrick Hackett,[2] Assistant Commissary of Issues........................... ————		5-28-1778	G.
240.	George A. Baker, Assistant Commissary of Issues........................... ————		5-28-1778	G.
241.	Bernard Sweeney, Assistant Commissary of Issues........................... ————		5-28-1778	G.
242.	Paul Percivale, Assistant Commissary of Issues............................ ————		5-28-1778	G.
243.	George Burroughs, Assistant Commissary of Issues........................... ————		5-28-1778	G.
244.	Thomas Wiley, Assistant Commissary of Issues............................ ————		5-28-1778	G.
245.	Michael Farley, Assistant Commissary of Issues............................ ————		5-28-1778	G.
246.	Benjamin Ballard, Assistant Commissary of Issues........................... ————		5-28-1778	G.
247.	Ebenezer Clark, Assistant Commissary of Issues........................... ————		5-28-1778	G.
248.	Robert Baugh, Assistant Commissary of Issues............................ ————		5-28-1778	G.
249.	James Gamble,[2] Assistant Commissary of Issues............................ ————		5-28-1778	G.
250.	Edward Lewis, Assistant Commissary of Issues............................ ————		5-28-1778	G.
251.	Joshua King, Forage Master............ ————		5-28-1778	G.

[1] From Pennsylvania.
[2] Oath taken at Bake House, Valley Forge.

Number	Deponent Office	Where taken	Date	Witness
252.	Dudley L. Chase, Brigade Quarter Master.	—	5-28-1778	G.
253.	Adam Gilchrist, Assistant to the Commissary General of Forage	—	5-28-1778	G.
254.	Charles Whittelsey, Brigade Quarter Master	—	5-28-1778	G.
255.	Samuel Kennedy, Senior Surgeon	—	5-26-1778	G.
256.	Nathan Wilkinson, Deputy Quarter Master General	—	5-23-1778	G.
257.	Samuel Morris,[1] Commissary General of Hospitals	—	5-26-1778	G.
258.	Abishai Thomas,[2] Deputy Quarter Master General	—	5-22-1778	G.
259.	James Rowney, Waggon Conductor	—	5-30-1778	G.
260.	Thomas Cole, Waggon Conductor	—	5-29-1778	G.
261.	Jacob Grace, Sub Waggon Conductor	—	5-30-1778	G.
262.	James Barclay, Waggon Conductor	—	5-29-1778	G.
263.	Noah Belole (Belote), Waggon Conductor.	—	5-29-1778	G.
264.	Henry Gordon, Waggon Conductor	—	5-29-1778	G.
265.	Josiah Kittera, Waggon Conductor	—	5-29-1778	G.
266.	John Lillie, Brigade Quarter Master	—	5-25-1778	G.
267.	John Shute,* Deputy Quarter Master General	—	5-26-1778	G.
268.	William Evans, Assistant Commissary of Purchases	—	6- 2-1778	—
269.	Joseph Dyer, Waggon Conductor	—	5-30-1778	G.
270.	John Ingram, Sub Conductor of Waggons.	—	5-29-1778	G.
271.	George Buyers, Sub Conductor of Waggons	—	5-29-1778	G.
272.	Thomas Crawford, Waggon Conductor	—	5-29-1778	G.
273.	James McCashlan, Sub Waggon Conductor	—	5-29-1778	G.
274.	Abraham Rand, Sub Waggon Conductor.	—	5-30-1778	G.
275.	William Gray, Waggon Conductor	—	5-29-1778	G.
276.	Francis Farron (Farrin), Sub Waggon Conductor	—	5-29-1778	G.
277.	James Williamson, Waggon Conductor	—	5-30-1778	G.
278.	James Williamson, Waggon Conductor	—	5-30-1778	G.
279.	Francis Farran (Farrin), Sub Waggon Conductor	—	5-29-1778	G.

[1] Affirmation.
[2] From North Carolina.
* Affirmation.

Number	Deponent Office	Where taken	Date	Witness
280.	James Yule, Deputy Waggon Master General	———	5-29-1778	G.
281.	Hugh McClaran, Waggon Conductor	———	5-30-1778	G.
282.	Stephen Eldredge, Sub Waggon Conductor	———	5-29-1778	G.
283.	Robert Riddle, Waggon Conductor	———	5-29-1778	G.

I *Charles Lee Major General* do acknowledge the UNITED STATES of AMERICA to be Free, Independent and Sovereign States, and declare that the people thereof owe no allegiance or obedience to George the Third, King of Great-Britain; and I renounce, refuse and abjure any allegiance or obedience to him; and I do *swear* that I will, to the utmost of my power, support, maintain and defend the said United States against the said King George the Third, his heirs and successors, and his or their abettors, assistants and adherents, and will serve the said United States in the office of *Majo: General* which I now hold, with fidelity, according to the best of my skill and understanding.

Sworn before me this 9 day of June 1778

G. Washington *Charles Lee*

Oath of Charles Lee.

I *John Ingram Sub Conductor of Waggons* do *swear* that I will faithfully, truly and impartially execute the office of *Sub Conductor of Waggons* to which I am appointed, and render a true account, when thereunto required, of all public monies by me received or expended, and of all stores or other effects to me intrusted, which belong to the UNITED STATES, and will, in all respects, discharge the trust reposed in me with justice and integrity, to the best of my skill and understanding.

Sworn the 29 May 1778 before me

Nath Greene MG *John Ingram*

Oath of Fidelity in Office taken by John Ingram.

Volume 166

RECORDS OF THE WAR DEPARTMENT

IN

THE NATIONAL ARCHIVES

Number	Deponent Office	Where taken	Date	Witness
284.	Thomas Cole, Waggon Conductor	—	5-29-1778	G.
285.	Joseph Dyre (Dyer), Waggon Conductor	—	5-30-1778	G.
286.	Joseph Hinderson, Waggon Conductor	—	5-29-1778	G.
287.	John J. Skidmore, Division Waggon Master	—	5-29-1778	G.
288.	Bodo Otto, Senior Surgeon, Middle Department	—	5-25-1778	G.
289.	Noah Belote (Belole), Waggon Conductor	—	5-29-1778	G.
290.	James Barclay (Bartley), Waggon Conductor	—	5-29-1778	G.
291.	Thomas Crawford, Waggon Conductor	—	5-29-1778	G.
292.	Ezekiel Brown, Surgeon	A	5-11-1778	T.C.
293.	Ebenezer Peabody, Lieutenant	A	5-11-1778	T.C.
294.	Joseph Charles, Ensign	A	5-11-1778	T.C.
295.	Jos. (or Jas.) Williams,* Captain	A	5-11-1778	T.C.
296.	Job Sumner,* Captain	A	5-11-1778	T.C.
297.	Charles Colton*	A	5-11-1778	T.C.
298.	Jabez Snow,* Lieutenant	A	5-11-1778	T.C.
299.	Isaac Gage,* Lieutenant	A	5-11-1778	T.C.
300.	Jno. Pownall,* Lieutenant	A	5-11-1778	T.C.
301.	Asa Coburn, Captain	A	5-11-1778	T.C.
302.	Samuel Pike,* Ensign	A	5-11-1778	T.C.
303.	Jonathan Maynard, Lieutenant	A	5-11-1778	T.C.
304.	Francis Stebbins, Ensign	A	5-11-1778	T.C.
305.	Benjamin Warren, Captain	A	5-11-1778	T.C.
306.	William Curtis, Lieutenant	A	5-11-1778	T.C.
307.	Luther Trowbridge, Lieutenant	A	5-11-1778	T.C.
308.	Robert Givens, Lieutenant	A	5-11-1778	T.C.
309.	Joseph Tucker, Ensign	A	5-11-1778	T.C.
310.	Elijah Day, Lieutenant	A	5-11-1778	T.C.
311.	James Lamb, First Steward of General Hospital of the Northern Department	A	5—-1778	T.C.
312.	James Lamb, (Oath not signed)	A	5—-1778	T.C.
313.	William May, Lieutenant Colonel	A	5-11-1778	T.C.
314.	Daniel Whiting, Major	A	5-11-1778	T.C.

* From Massachusetts.

34 OATHS OF ALLEGIANCE

Number	Deponent	Office	Where taken	Date	Witness
315.	Daniel Lane, Captain	A		5-11-1778	J.S.
316.	Jonathan Loring,* Lieutenant Colonel	A		5-11-1778	T.C.
317.	Abijah Richardson,* Surgeon's Mate	A		5-11-1778	T.C.
318.	William McKendry, Quarter Master	A		5-11-1778	T.C.
319.	William Cheney,* Adjutant	A		5-11-1778	T.C.
320.	Daniel Lane, Captain	A		——	—
321.	Benjamin Billings, Lieutenant	A		5-11-1778	T.C.
322.	Luke Day, Captain	A		5-11-1778	T.C.
323.	William White, Adjutant	A		5-11-1778	T.C.
324.	William Hudson Ballard, Captain	A		5-11-1778	T.C.
325.	James Lunt, Lieutenant	A		5-11-1778	T.C.
326.	Levi Parker, Ensign	A		5-11-1778	T.C.
327.	William Patrick, Captain	A		5-11-1778	T.C.
328.	Eliphalet Thorp, Lieutenant	A		5-11-1778	T.C.
329.	Ichabod Alden, Colonel		——	——	—.
330.	Samuel Buffinton, Lieutenant	A		5-11-1778	T.C.
331.	Stephen Carter, Lieutenant	A		5-11-1778	T.C.
332.	Aaron Holden, Lieutenant	A		5-11-1778	T.C.
333.	Samuel Tuthill,* Lieutenant	A		5-11-1778	T.C.
334.	Jno. Maynard,* Lieutenant	A		5-11-1778	T.C.
335.	Jno. Smith,* Ensign	A		5-11-1778	T.C.
336.	Francis Stebbins,* Ensign	A		5-11-1778	T.C.
337.	Jno. Meacham,* Ensign	A		5-11-1778	T.C.
338.	Henry Savage,* Ensign	A		5-11-1778	T.C.
339.	Daniel Lee,* Lieutenant	A		5-11-1778	T.C.
340.	James Davis,* Lieutenant	A		5-11-1778	T.C.
341.	Samuel Burnham,* Lieutenant	A		5-11-1778	T.C.
342.	Samuel Day,* Lieutenant	A		5-11-1778	T.C.
343.	Robert Oliver,* Major	A		5-11-1778	T.C.
344.	Samuel Hawes,* Captain	A		5-11-1778	T.C.
345.	Edward Cumpston,* Captain	A		5-11-1778	T.C.
346.	James Tisdale,* Lieutenant	A		5-11-1778	T.C.
347.	Thomas Pritch,* Lieutenant	A		5-11-1778	T.C.
348.	Theo. M. Bland, Colonel		——	10-21-1778	W.
349.	James Black, Captain	VF		5-11-1778	S.
350.	Daniel Nivon (Nivans), Captain	VF		5-11-1778	S.
351.	Robert Hunter, Ensign	VF		5-11-1778	S.
352.	Joshua Drake, Lieutenant	VF		5-11-1778	S.
353.	Richard Oliver, Lieutenant	VF		5-11-1778	S.
354.	Patrick Cronen, Quarter Master	VF		5-11-1778	S.
355.	Hugh Peacock, Lieutenant	VF		5-11-1778	S.
356.	Alexander Dow, Lieutenant	VF		5-11-1778	S.

* From Massachusetts.

RECORDS OF THE WAR DEPARTMENT—VOL. 166   35

Number	Deponent	Office	Where taken	Date	Witness
357.	Anthony Maxwell,	Ensign	VF	5-11-1778	S.
358.	Peter Taulman (Tallman),	Adjutant	VF	5-11-1778	S.
359.	Daniel Wood,	Lieutenant	VF	5-11-1778	S.
360.	Edward Armstrong,	Lieutenant	VF	5-11-1778	S.
361.	John Sandford,	Captain	VF	5-11-1778	S.
362.	David Kirkpatrick,	Ensign	VF	5-23-1778	S.
363.	Nathaniel Tom,	Captain	VF	5-23-1778	S.
364.	James Monell,	Lieutenant	VF	5-23-1778	S.
365.	Jonathan Lawrence,	Lieutenant	VF	5-23-1778	S.
366.	Abraham Neely (Neily),	Lieutenant	VF	5-23-1778	S.
367.	Finch Gildersleeve,	Ensign	VF	5—-1778	S.
368.	Daniel Morgan,	Colonel	R	6-10-1778	K.
369.	James Knox,	Captain	R	6-10-1778	K.
370.	Gabriel Long,	Captain	R	6-10-1778	K.
371.	Alexander Martin,	First Lieutenant	R	6-10-1778	K.
372.	James Culbertson,	First Lieutenant	R	6-10-1778	K.
373.	John Hardin (Harding),	First Lieutenant	R	6-10-1778	K.
374.	Benjamin Taliaferro,	Captain	R	6-10-1778	K.
375.	Charles McCarter,	Surgeon	R	6-10-1778	K.
376.	Henry Hanly (Henly),	Quarter Master	R	6-10-1778	K.
377.	Reuben Long,	Ensign	R	6-10-1778	K.
378.	William Stevens (Stephens),	Ensign	R	6-10-1778	K.
379.	John Colman,	Adjutant	R	6-10-1778	K.
380.	Elijah Evans,	Second Lieutenant	R	6-10-1778	K.
381.	Thomas Boyd,	Second Lieutenant	R	6-10-1778	K.
382.	Benjamin Ashby,	Second Lieutenant	R	6-10-1778	K.
383.	John Lapsley,	Second Lieutenant	R	6-10-1778	K.
384.	William Lewis Lovely,	Second Lieutenant	R	6-10-1778	K.
385.	James Parr,	Captain	R	6-10-1778	K.
386.	Chiswell Barret,	Cornet	R	6-10-1778	K.
387.	Samuel Tenny,	Surgeon	VF	5-13-1778	V.
388.	Jonathan Knight,	Surgeon's Mate	VF	5-24-1778	V.
389.	David Adams,	Surgeon	VF	5-24-1778	V.
390.	John Viol,	Ensign	VF	5-14-1778	V.
391.	John Strong,	Ensign	VF	5-13-1778	V.
392.	Lebbens Loomis,	Ensign	VF	5-13-1778	V.
393.	Aaron Benjamin,	Ensign	VF	5-24-1778	V.
394.	Daniel Wait,	Lieutenant	VF	5-23-1778	V.
395.	Charles Fanning,	Lieutenant	VF	5-23-1778	V.
396.	David Johnson,	Lieutenant	VF	5-14-1778	V.
397.	Samuel Arnold,	Lieutenant	VF	5-14-1778	V.
398.	Daniel C. Tillinghast,	Ensign	VF	5-14-1778	V.
399.	John Durkee,	Lieutenant	VF	5-13-1778	V.

36 OATHS OF ALLEGIANCE

Number	Deponent	Office	Where taken	Date	Witness
400.	Seth Phelps, Lieutenant		VF	5-13-1778	V.
401.	Silas Holt, Lieutenant		VF	5-13-1778	V.
402.	Lemuel Cleft, Lieutenant		VF	5-13-1778	V.
403.	Timothy Cleveland, Lieutenant		VF	5-13-1778	V.
404.	Uriah Mitchell, Brigade Quarter Master		VF	6- 1-1778	V.
405.	Daniel Barnes, Lieutenant		VF	5-13-1778	V.
406.	Alexander Mack (Meek), Lieutenant		VF	5-24-1778	V.
407.	Ebenezer West, Lieutenant		VF	5-31-1778	V.
408.	Nathan P. Jackson, Lieutenant		VF	5-24-1778	V.
409.	Asahel Hodge, Lieutenant		VF	5-24-1778	V.
410.	Bildad Granger, Lieutenant		VF	5-24-1778	V.
411.	Robert Durkee, Captain		VF	5-24-1778	V.
412.	Simon Spalding, Lieutenant		VF	5-24-1778	V.
413.	David Judson, Lieutenant		VF	5-24-1778	V.
414.	Oliver Jencks, Lieutenant		VF	5-24-1778	V.
415.	Nathaniel Bishop, Lieutenant		VF	5-26-1778	V.
416.	Timothy Pierce, Lieutenant		VF	5-24-1778	V.
417.	Nathan Weeks, Lieutenant		VF	5-24-1778	V.
418.	Selah Benton, Lieutenant		VF	5-23-1778	V.
419.	Edmund Coleman, Lieutenant		VF	5-24-1778	V.
420.	Nehemiah Rice (Royce), Captain		VF	5-14-1778	V.
421.	John Harmon, Captain		VF	5-19-1778	V.
422.	Andrew Fitch, Captain		VF	5-14-1778	V.
423.	Thomas Arnold, Captain		VF	5-14-1778	V.
424.	Samuel Comstock, Captain		VF	5-14-1778	V.
425.	Robert Hallam, Captain		VF	5-14-1778	V.
426.	Sylvanus Brown, Captain		VF	5-14-1778	V.
427.	Thomas Hughes, Captain		VF	5-13-1778	V.
428.	Beriah Bill, Captain		VF	5-13-1778	V.
429.	William Tew, Captain		VF	5-30-1778	V.
430.	Ebenezer Flagg, Captain		VF	5-13-1778	V.
431.	David Smith, Captain		VF	5-13-1778	V.
432.	Samuel Sanford, Captain		VF	5-13-1778	V.
433.	Paul Brigham, Captain		VF	5-13-1778	V.
434.	Samuel Mattocks, Captain		VF	5-13-1778	V.
435.	Theophilus Manson, Captain		VF	5-23-1778	V.
436.	Jonathan Wallen, Captain		VF	5-24-1778	V.
437.	William Allen, Captain		VF	5-24-1778	V.
438.	Simeon Thayer, Major		VF	5-13-1778	—.
439.	Joseph Hoit (Hoyt), Major		VF	5-13-1778	V.
440.	John Sumner, Major		VF	5-14-1778	V.
441.	Jeremiah Olney, Lieutenant Colonel		VF	5-13-1778	V.
442.	Jacob Wale (Wales), Captain		VF	5-18-1778	P.

RECORDS OF THE WAR DEPARTMENT—VOL. 166

Number	Deponent Office	Where taken	Date	Witness
443.	Jonathan Turner, First Lieutenant	VF	5-28-1778	P.
444.	Asa Pixley, Ensign	Camp	5-30-1778	P.
445.	Silas Clark, Lieutenant	VF	5-18-1778	P.
446.	Josiah Parsons, Lieutenant	W.P.	8-24-1778	P.
447.	John Littlefield, Ensign	W.P.	8-24-1778	P.
448.	Othniel Taylor, Lieutenant	K.F.	7-15-1778	P.
449.	Daniel Brown, Ensign	VF	5-22-1778	P.
450.	Samuel Buss, Lieutenant	VF	5-13-1778	P.
451.	Levi Dodge, Ensign	VF	5-13-1778	P.
452.	Reuben Dodge, Ensign	VF	5-19-1778	P.
453.	William Warner, Captain	VF	5-13-1778	P.
454.	Elisha Skinner, Surgeon	VF	5-13-1778	P.
455.	Nathan Parsons, Adjutant	VF	5-13-1778	P.
456.	James Buxton, Ensign	VF	5-18-1778	P.
457.	Philip Thomas, Captain	VF	5-13-1778	P.
458.	Christopher Marshall, Captain	VF	5-13-1778	P.
459.	Elnathan Haskell, Major	VF	5-11-1778	P.
460.	Benjamin Tupper, Colonel	VF	5-11-1778	P.
461.	Nathaniel Coit Allen, Paymaster	VF	5-13-1778	P.
462.	Thomas Cummings, Lieutenant	VF	5-15-1778	P.
463.	Nathaniel Winslow, Major	VF	5-11-1778	P.
464.	David Farnum, Lieutenant	VF	5-18-1778	P.
465.	Asa Bullard, Ensign	VF	5-30-1778	P.
466.	Daniel Lunt, Lieutenant	VF	5-18-1778	P.
467.	Joshua Bramhall, Ensign	VF	5-11-1778	P.
468.	Jonathan Haskell, Ensign	VF	5-11-1778	P.
469.	Josiah Smith, Captain	VF	6-12-1778	P.
470.	Samuel Carlton, Lieutenant Colonel	—	—	—.
471.	Tobias Fernald, Major	Rdg	2-21-1778	T.M.
472.	Peleg Turner, Quarter Master	N.B.	7- 3-1778	P.
473.	Samuel Brewer, Colonel	VF	5-11-1778	P.
474.	Joseph Gardiner, Surgeon's Mate	VF	5-11-1778	P.
475.	Daniel Merrill, Captain	VF	5-11-1778	P.
476.	Nathan Watkins, Captain	VF	5-11-1778	P.
477.	James Donnell, Captain	Camp	5-11-1778	P.
478.	John Whiting, Quarter Master	Camp	5-11-1778	P.
479.	Timothy Remick, Lieutenant Colonel	VF	5-11-1778	P.
480.	William Frost, First Lieutenant	VF	5-11-1778	—.
481.	John Wingate, Surgeon	VF	5-11-1778	P.
482.	Abraham Williams, Lieutenant	VF	5-19-1778	P.
483.	Luke Hitchcock, Lieutenant	VF	5-19-1778	P.
484.	James Means, Lieutenant	VF	5-19-1778	P.
485.	William Batman, Adjutant	VF	5-11-1778	P.

Number	Deponent Office	Where taken	Date	Witness
486.	Ebenezer Stevens, Lieutenant	VF	5-11-1778	P.
487.	Ebenezer Storer, Ensign	VF	5-11-1778	P.
488.	David Watts, First Lieutenant	VF	5-11-1778	P.
489.	Joshua Nason, Ensign	VF	5-11-1778	P.
490.	John Hubble (Hubbell), Ensign	VF	5-11-1778	P.
491.	Joshua Nason, Ensign	VF	5-11-1778	P.
492.	John Pray, Lieutenant Colonel	VF	5-11-1778	P.
493.	Andrew Englis, Lieutenant	VF	5-11-1778	P.
494.	John Buck, Ensign	VF	5-11-1778	P.
495.	Richard Mayberry, Captain	VF	5-11-1778	P.
496.	Daniel Wheelwright, Captain	VF	5-11-1778	P.
497.	Lemuel Miller, Lieutenant	VF	6- 6-1778	P.
498.	Henry Sewall, First Lieutenant & Muster Master	VF	6- 6-1778	P.
499.	Jonathan Libby, Ensign	VF	6- 4-1778	P.
500.	George White, Captain	VF	5-18-1778	P.
501.	Samuel Page, Captain	VF	5-18-1778	P.
502.	Billy Porter, Captain	VF	5-18-1778	P.
503.	Moses Greenleaf, Captain	VF	5-18-1778	P.
504.	William Hasty, Lieutenant	VF	5-18-1778	P.
505.	John Francis, Adjutant	VF	5-18-1778	P.
506.	John Jones, Surgeon's Mate	VF	5-18-1778	P.
507.	Hugh Mulloy, Ensign	VF	5-18-1778	P.
508.	Isaac Childs, Lieutenant	VF	5-18-1778	P.
509.	Nehemiah Emerson, Ensign	VF	5-18-1778	P.
510.	Zebulon King, Lieutenant	VF	5-19-1778	P.
511.	Joseph Foot, Lieutenant	Camp	5-30-1778	P.
512.	Jonathan Conant, Paymaster	VF	6- 5-1778	P.
513.	Aaron Francis, Quarter Master	VF	6- 7-1778	P.
514.	William McKenney, Ensign	VF	6- 1-1778	P.
515.	Joshua Eddy, Captain	Camp	6-11-1778	P.
516.	Benjamin Shaw, Ensign	VF	6- 1-1778	P.
517.	Samuel Goodrich, Lieutenant	VF	5-18-1778	P.
518.	William Burley, Lieutenant	VF	6- 1-1778	P.
519.	Joseph Bates, Lieutenant	VF	5-11-1778	P.
520.	Joseph Wadsworth, Captain	VF	5-19-1778	P.
521.	Samuel Tubbs, Major	VF	5-19-1778	P.
522.	Crocker Sampson, Quarter Master	VF	5-19-1778	P.
523.	Adam Fish, Lieutenant	VF	5-27-1778	P.
524.	John Lesuer, Ensign	VF	5-27-1778	P.
525.	Gamaliel Bradford, Colonel	VF	--13-1778	P.
526.	Barachiah Bassett, Lieutenant Colonel	VF	5-11-1778	P.
527.	Zebedee Redding, Captain	VF	5-11-1778	P.

RECORDS OF THE WAR DEPARTMENT—VOL. 166

Number	Deponent Office	Where taken	Date	Witness
528.	Samuel Finley, Surgeon	VF	5-11-1778	P.
529.	William Beach (Beech), Lieutenant	VF	5-11-1778	S.
530.	Benjamin Weatherby, Captain	VF	5-11-1778	S.
531.	James Brodrick, Captain	VF	5-11-1778	S.
532.	John Davey, Surgeon's Mate	VF	5-11-1778	S.
533.	William Bull, Lieutenant	VF	5-11-1778	S.
534.	Nathaniel Ogden, Quarter Master	VF	5-11-1778	S.
535.	John Orr, Lieutenant	VF	5-11-1778	S.
536.	Uzal Meeker, Lieutenant	VF	5-11-1778	S.
537.	John Hammitt, Lieutenant	VF	5-11-1778	S.
538.	Richard Edsall, Captain	VF	5-11-1778	S.
539.	Oliver Spencer, Colonel	VF	5-11-1778	S.
540.	Barne Ogden, Lieutenant	VF	5-11-1778	S.
541.	Godfried Schwartz,[1] Lieutenant	Camp	5-11-1778	M.
542.	Marcus Young,[1] Lieutenant	Camp	5-11-1778	M.
543.	Bernard Hubley,[1] Lieutenant	Camp	5-11-1778	M.
544.	David Morgan,[1] Ensign	Camp	5-11-1778	M.
545.	Michael Bayer,[1] Lieutenant	Camp	5-11-1778	M.
546.	Henry Maag (Magg),[1] Ensign	Camp	5-11-1778	M.
547.	William Hayser (Heiser),[1] Captain	Camp	5-11-1778	M.
548.	Jacob Bunner,[1] Captain	———	5-11-1778	M.
549.	Jacob Cramer,[1] Lieutenant	Camp	5-11-1778	M.
550.	Daniel Burkhard,[1] Major	Camp	5-11-1778	M.
551.	Charles Baltzell,[1] Captain	Camp	5-12-1778	M.
552.	Thomas Edison,[1] Lieutenant	Camp	5-12-1778	M.
553.	Henry Shrupp,[1] Ensign	Camp	5-12-1778	M.
554.	John Henry, Captain	AP	6-12-1778	K.
555.	Ludwick Weltner, Lieutenant Colonel	———	6-15-1778	M.
556.	Philip Shrawder,[1] Lieutenant	VF	5-23-1778	M.
557.	Edward Prall,[2] Captain	Camp	5-28-1778	M.
558.	Martin Shugart,[1] Second Lieutenant	Camp	6- 1-1778	M.
559.	Jeronemus Hoogland, Adjutant	———	8- 1-1778	S.
560.	Henry Miller, Chaplain	Camp	5-25-1778	M.
561.	William Stanton, Paymaster	———	8-19-1778	S.
562.	Zebulon Pike, Cornet	W.P.	8-18-1778	S.
563.	Robert Yancy, Cornet	Camp	8-18-1778	S.
564.	Peter Manifold, Cornet	W.P.	8-18-1778	S.
565.	John Hinderson, Cornet	———	8-18-1778	S.
566.	Larkin Dorsey, Cornet	———	8-18-1778	S.
567.	John Craig, Lieutenant	———	8-18-1778	S.
568.	Robert Rose, Surgeon	Camp	8-18-1778	S.

[1] Member of the German Battalion.
[2] From Maryland.

40   OATHS OF ALLEGIANCE

Number	Deponent	Office	Where taken	Date	Witness
569.	Thomas Harrison McCalla, Surgeon.....	———	8-18-1778	S.
570.	Samuel Williamson, Chaplain...........	W.P.	8-18-1778	S.
571.	John Hughes,[1] Quarter Master.........	W.P.	8-18-1778	S.
572.	Andrew Nixon, Adjutant...............	———	8-18-1778	S.
573.	John Watts, Lieutenant................	———	8-18-1778	S.
574.	George Gray, Captain,................	W.P.	8-18-1778	S.
575.	Alexander S. Dandridge, Captain.......	Camp	8-18-1778	S.
576.	Richard Call, Captain.................	W.P.	8-18-1778	S.
577.	John Heard, Jr., Captain...............	W.P.	8-18-1778	S.
578.	David Plunket, Captain...............	Camp	8-18-1778	S.
579.	Nicholas Ruxton Moore, Captain.......	Camp	8-18-1778	S.
580.	William Washington, Major............	———	8-18-1778	S.
581.	Churchill Jones, Captain..............	Camp	8-18-1778	S.
582.	John Jameson, Major..................	Camp	8-18-1778	S.
583.	Anthony W. White, Lieutenant Colonel..	Camp	8-18-1778	S.
584.	Stephen Moylan, Colonel..............	W.P.	8-18-1778	S.
585.	John Swan, Captain...................	W.P.	9- 8-1778	S.
586.	John Shethar, Captain................	W.P.	8- 2-1778	S.
587.	Benjamin Temple, Lieutenant Colonel...	W.P.	9-15-1778	S.
588.	John Robert, First Lieutenant.........	VF	6- 8-1778	S.
589.	Jonah Hallett, Second Lieutenant......	VF	6- 8-1778	S.
590.	Albert Pawling, Major................	VF	6- 8-1778	S.
591.	Aaron Burr, Lieutenant Colonel........	VF	6- 8-1778	S.
592.	Joseph Savage, Lieutenant.............	Hld	6-17-1778	H.
593.	David Parsons, Captain...............	Hld	6-17-1778	H.
594.	Thomas Anderson, Quarter Master.....	W.P.	9-15-1778	H.
595.	Abner Prior, Captain.................	W.P.	9-15-1778	H.
596.	David Dorrance, First Lieutenant......	W.P.	9-15-1778	H.
597.	John Armstrong,* Lieutenant..........	———	2-28-1778	St.C.

[1] From Virginia.
* From Pennsylvania.

I Zebulon Pike do Acknowledge the United States of America to be free Independent & Sovereign States & Declare that the People thereof Owe no Alegience or Obedience to George the Third King of Great Britain & I Renounce Refuse & Abjure any Alegience or Obedience to him & I do Swear that I will to the Utmost of my Power Support & Defend the s.d United States Against the Said King George the Third his heirs & Successors & his or their Abettors Assistants & Adherents & will Serve the Said United States in the Office of Cornet Which I now hold with Fidelity According to the best of my Skill & Understanding —

Sworn Before me at White Plains
this 10th day of August 1778   Zebulon Pike Cornet

Stirling Major Gen.l

This Oath is especially interesting because it was evidently written by Zebulon Pike himself and then Lord Stirling added the statement that it was sworn to before him at White Plains.

Volume 167

RECORDS OF THE WAR DEPARTMENT
IN
THE NATIONAL ARCHIVES

Number   Deponent   Office   Where taken   Date   Witness

1. William Kersey,* Second Lieutenant.....VF..........5-11-1778..S.
2. William Gifford,* Captain...............VF..........5-11-1778..S.
3. Francis Barber,* Lieutenant Colonel.....VF..........5-11-1778..S.
4. Jos. T. Anderson,* Captain..............VF..........5-11-1889..S.
5. John Mott,* Captain.....................VF..........5-11-1778..S.
6. Ephriam Loree,* Surgeon's Mate.........VF..........5-11-1778..S.
7. Nathan Wilkinson,* Second Lieutenant...VF..........5-11-1778..S.
8. Thomas Patterson,* Captain.............VF..........5-11-1778..S.
9. Richard Cox,* Captain..................VF..........5-11-1778..S.
10. Joseph Bloomfield,* Major..............VF..........5-11-1778..S.
11. Edmund Disney Thomas,* First Lieutenant..............................VF..........5-11-1778..S.
12. John Reading,* First Lieutenant........VF..........5-11-1778..S.
13. Samuel Shippard (Sheppard),* Adjutant..VF..........5-11-1778..S.
14. Benjamin Horn,* Second Lieutenant.....VF..........5-11-1778..S.
15. Aaron Day,* Second Lieutenant.........VF..........5-11-1778..S.
16. Jeremiah Ballard,* Captain.............VF..........5-21-1778..S.
17. John B. Niker,* Surgeon................VF..........5-11-1778..S.
18. Samuel Conn,* Second Lieutenant.......VF..........5-11-1778..S.
19. Absm. Martin,* Paymaster..............VF..........5-11-1778..S.
20. Ephm. Whitlock,* Second Lieutenant....VF..........5-11-1778..S.
21. Samuel F. Parker,* Muster Master......VF..........5-11-1778..S.
22. David Brearly,* Lieutenant Colonel......VF..........5-11-1778..S.
23. Seth Johnson,* First Lieutenant.........VF..........5-11-1778..S.
24. Alexander Mitchell,* Captain...........VF..........5-11-1778..S.
25. Ephriam Martin,* Colonel...............VF..........5-11-1778..S.
26. Abel Weymon,* First Lieutenant........VF..........5-11-1778..S.
27. Jonathan Forman,* Captain.............VF..........5-11-1778..S.
28. Abraham Lyon,* Captain................VF..........5-11-1778..S.
29. John Conway,* Major....................VF..........5-11-1778..S.
30. Andrew Hunter,* Chaplain..............VF..........5-11-1778..S.
31. Wessel T. Stout,* Second Lieutenant....VF..........5-11-1778..S.
32. Jacob Harris,* Surgeon's Mate..........VF..........5-11-1778..S.
33. Absolem Bonham (Bonum),* Lieutenant..VF..........5-11-1778..S.
34. Stephen Billing, Lieutenant.............VF..........5-29-1778..V.

* From New Jersey.

Number	Deponent Office	Where taken	Date	Witness
35.	Thomas Converse, Captain	VF	5-29-1778	V.
36.	Phineas Beardsley (Bardsley), Captain	VF	5-29-1778	V.
37.	Tryal Tanner, Adjutant	VF	5-25-1778	V.
38.	Ephriam Chamberlin, Lieutenant	VF	5-29-1778	V.
39.	Augustine Taylor, Lieutenant	VF	5-29-1778	V.
40.	Theodore Woodbridge, Captain	VF	5-29-1778	V.
41.	Philemon Hall, Ensign	VF	5-29-1778	V.
42.	Isaac Keeler, Ensign	VF	5-13-1778	V.
43.	Samuel Barnum, Lieutenant	VF	5-29-1778	V.
44.	James Barnes, Lieutenant	VF	5-29-1778	V.
45.	Caleb Baldwin, First Lieutenant	VF	5-25-1778	V.
46.	Titus Watson, Captain	VF	5-29-1778	V.
47.	John Ellis, Chaplain	VF	5-30-1778	V.
48.	John Hollenbeak, First Lieutenant	VF	5-29-1778	V.
49.	Josiah Starr, Colonel	VF	5-29-1778	V.
50.	Stephen Hall, Captain	VF	5-29-1778	V.
51.	Phineas Grover, Lieutenant	VF	5-21-1778	V.
52.	Charles Miel, Lieutenant	VF	5-29-1778	V.
53.	Ebenezer Hills, Captain	VF	5-31-1778	V.
54.	Jos. (or Jas.) Willcox, Second Lieutenant	VF	5-29-1778	V.
55.	Aaron Stevens, Captain	VF	5-29-1778	V.
56.	Hezekiah Rogers, Adjutant	VF	5-13-1778	V.
57.	Jabez Smith, Surgeon's Mate	VF	5-31-1778	V.
58.	Heman Swift, Colonel	VF	5-25-1778	V.
59.	Jonathan Johnson, Major	VF	5-13-1778	V.
60.	Edward Palmer, Lieutenant	VF	5-13-1778	V.
61.	Joseph Allyn Wright, Captain	VF	5-13-1778	V.
62.	Jasper Mead, Quarter Master	VF	5-13-1778	V.
63.	Daniel Bradley, Ensign	VF	5-13-1778	V.
64.	Jabez Smith, Surgeon's Mate	VF	5-13-1778	V.
65.	Cornelius Higgins, Lieutenant	VF	5-13-1778	V.
66.	Cornelius Russell, Lieutenant	VF	5-13-1778	V.
67.	William Henshaw, Lieutenant	VF	5-13-1778	V.
68.	Samuel Hait, Captain	VF	5-13-1778	V.
69.	Eli Catlin, Captain	VF	5-13-1778	V.
70.	Roger Wadsworth, Lieutenant	VF	5-13-1778	V.
71.	Solomon Strong, Captain	VF	5-13-1778	V.
72.	Elijah Chapman, Lieutenant	VF	5-30-1778	V.
73.	William Green, Lieutenant	VF	5-13-1778	V.
74.	Josiah Child, Captain	VF	5-30-1778	V.
75.	Job Smith, Paymaster	VF	5-31-1778	V.
76.	Thaddeus Keeler, Second Lieutenant	VF	5-13-1778	V.
77.	John St. John, Lieutenant	VF	5-13-1778	V.

Oaths of Allegiance

Number	Deponent Office	Where taken	Date	Witness
78.	Josiah Lacy, Captain	VF	5-13-1778	V.
79.	Matthew Mead, Lieutenant Colonel	VF	5-13-1778	V.
80.	Hezekiah Tracy, Second Lieutenant	VF	5-13-1778	V.
81.	Richard Douglass, First Lieutenant	VF	5-13-1778	V.
82.	Ezra Lee, Second Lieutenant	VF	5-13-1778	V.
83.	James Lord, Second Lieutenant	VF	5-13-1778	V.
84.	Henry Hill, First Lieutenant	VF	5-13-1778	V.
85.	John Tiffany, Second Lieutenant	VF	5-13-1778	V.
86.	Simeon Avery, Second Lieutenant	VF	5-13-1778	V.
87.	Samuel Brown, Surgeon's Mate	VF	5-13-1778	V.
88.	Ezra Selden, Adjutant	VF	5-13-1778	V.
89.	Ichabod Spencer, Ensign	VF	5-13-1778	V.
90.	Enoch Reed, First Lieutenant	VF	5-13-1778	V.
91.	Omitted.			
92.	Darius Peck, Second Lieutenant	VF	5-23-1778	V.
93.	John Shumway, Captain	VF	5-13-1778	V.
94.	Ebenezer Perkins, Captain	VF	5-13-1778	V.
95.	William Richards, Captain	VF	5-13-1778	V.
96.	Ithamer Harvey, Captain	VF	5-13-1778	V.
97.	Eliphalet Holmes, Captain	VF	5-13-1778	V.
98.	Roger Alden, Major of Brigade	VF	5-13-1778	V.
99.	Jedidiah Huntington, Brigadier General	VF	6- 2-1778	V.
100.	Moses Cleveland, Lieutenant	VF	5- 1-1778	V.
101.	Nathaniel Chipman, Lieutenant	VF	5-13-1778	V.
102.	James Beebee, Captain	VF	5-13-1778	V.
103.	James Andrews, Second Lieutenant	VF	5-13-1778	V.
104.	Benjamin Perry,[1] Surgeon	——	5-12-1778	W.
105.	Benjamin Boyer,[1] First Lieutenant	——	5-12-1778	W.
106.	John Patterson,[1] Captain	——	5-12-1778	W.
107.	Peter Gosner,[1] Captain	——	——-——	W.
108.	Henry Miller,[1] Lieutenant Colonel	——	——-——	W.
109.	Solomon Fenton, Second Lieutenant	VF	5-13-1778	V.
110.	Charles Stewart, Ensign	VF	5-13-1778	V.
111.	Benoni Shipman, First Lieutenant	VF	5-13-1778	V.
112.	Peter Robertson, First Lieutenant	VF	5-15-1778	V.
113.	Isaac Day, Surgeon's Mate	VF	6-13-1778	H.
114.	Isaac Turner, First Lieutenant	VF	5-13-1778	V.
115.	John Mills, Captain	VF	5-13-1778	V.
116.	Stephen Betts, Captain	VF	5-30-1778	V.
1¹7.	Ames Walbridge, Captain	VF	5-13-1778	V.
11.	Thomas Callender,[2] Lieutenant	——	5-24-1778	McI.

[1] From Pennsylvania.
[2] From North Carolina.

RECORDS OF THE WAR DEPARTMENT—VOL. 167   45

Number	Deponent Office	Where taken	Date	Witness
119.	James Ninier,[2] Lieutenant	—	5-14-1778	McI.
120.	Henry Ten Eyck, Adjutant	VF	5-13-1778	V.
121.	Isaac Sherman, Lieutenant Colonel	VF	5-23-1778	V.
122.	William Hilton,[2] First Lieutenant	—	5-12-1778	McI.
123.	Robert Varner,[2] Lieutenant	—	5-19-1778	McI.
124.	Frederick Heimberg,[2] Surgeon	—	5-19-1778	McI.
125.	James Read,[2] Captain	—	5-14-1778	McI.
126.	Anthony Sharp,[2] Captain	—	5-14-1778	McI.
127.	James Craven,[2] Lieutenant	—	5-19-1778	McI.
128.	William Slade,[2] Lieutenant	—	5-14-1778	McI.
129.	Stephen Slade,[2] Quarter Master	—	5-19-1778	McI.
130.	Charles Girard,[2] Lieutenant	—	5-14-1778	McI.
131.	Lachlan McIntosh, Jr.,[3] Captain	VF	5-12-1778	McI.
132.	John Scull,[2] First Lieutenant	—	5-12-1778	McI.
133.	Charles Stewart,[2] Lieutenant	—	5-12-1778	McI.
134.	John Craddock,[2] Captain	—	5-19-1778	McI.
135.	Kedar Ballard,[2] Captain	—	5-12-1778	McI.
136.	Samuel Jones,[2] Second Lieutenant	—	5—-1778	McI.
137.	Arthur Cotgrave,[2] Second Lieutenant	—	5-12-1778	McI.
138.	Francis Tartanson,[2] Captain	—	5-11-1778	McI.
139.	Clement Hall,[2] Captain	—	5-11-1778	McI.
140.	Manlove Tarrant,[2] Captain	—	5-11-1778	McI.
141.	John Ingles,[2] Captain	—	5-11-1778	McI.
142.	Patrick McGibboney,[2] Lieutenant	—	5-17-1778	McI.
143.	Robert Council,[2] Second Lieutenant	—	5-12-1778	McI.
144.	Richard Anderson,[2] Second Lieutenant	—	5-12-1778	McI.
145.	John Roberts,[2] First Lieutenant	—	5—-1778	McI.
146.	John Rice,[2] Lieutenant	—	5-11-1778	McI.
147.	Benjamin Williams,[2] Captain	—	5-11-1778	McI.
148.	William Sheppard,[2] Captain	—	5—-1778	McI.
149.	Thomas Armstrong,[2] Captain	—	5-11-1778	McI.
150.	William Fenner,[2] Major	—	5-11-1778	McI.
151.	Hardy Murfree (Murphy),[2] Major	—	5-11-1778	McI.
152.	Selby Harney,[2] Lieutenant Colonel	—	5—-1778	McI.
153.	John Sheppard,[2] Major	—	5-11-1778	McI.
154.	John Harrison,[2] Major	—	5-11-1778	McI.
155.	Robert Bebane,[2] Lieutenant Colonel	—	5-11-1778	McI.
156.	Benjamin Coleman,[2] Captain	—	5-11-1778	McI.
157.	Thomas Clark,[2] Colonel	—	5-11-1778	McI.
158.	Abraham Sheppard,[2] Colonel	—	5-11-1778	McI.
159.	Charles Coleman,[2] Quarter Master	—	5-20-1778	McI.

[2] From North Carolina.
[3] From Georgia.

46   OATHS OF ALLEGIANCE

| Number | Deponent Office | Where taken | Date | Witness |

160. James Coots,[2] Lieutenant............... ———.......5-20-1778..McI.
161. William Womack,[2] Quarter Master...... ———.......5-20-1778..McI.
162. Joshua Bowman,[2] Captain............... ———.......5-20-1778..McI.
163. Griffith John McKee (McKree),[2] Captain.———.......5-20-1778..McI.
164. Stephen Owen,[2] First Lieutenant........ ———.......5-15-1778..McI.
165. Philip Taylor,[2] Captain.................. ———.......5-20-1778..McI.
166. Peter Bacot,[2] Lieutenant................ ———.......5-21-1778..McI.
167. William McCluer,[2] Surgeon.............. ———.......5-21-1778..McI.
168. John Brown,[2] Captain................... ———.......5-21-1778..McI.
169. William Terrill,[2] Lieutenant............. ———.......5-21-1778..McI.
170. William Walton,[2] Lieutenant............ ———.......5-16-1778..McI.
171. William Armstrong,[2] Captain........... ———.......5-16-1778..McI.
172. James Campbell,[2] Lieutenant........... ———.......5-16-1778..McI.
173. John Patten,[2] Colonel................... ———.......5-11-1778..McI.
174. Thomas Pasteur,[2] Ensign................ ———.......5-16-1778..McI.
175. William Goodman,[2] Captain............ ———.......5-16-1778..McI.
176. Adam Boyd,[2] Chaplain..................VF.........5-16-1778..McI.
177. Robert Fenner,[2] Captain................ ———.......5-15-1778..McI.
178. Samuel Hanson,[2] Surgeon to his Excel-
     lency's Guard........................ ———.......5-15-1778..McI.
179. Thomas Finny,[2] Lieutenant............. ———.......5-15-1778..McI.
180. Samuel Budd,[2] Lieutenant.............. ———.......5-15-1778..McI.
181. Joseph Ferebee,[2] Lieutenant............ ———.......5-15-1778..McI.
182. Joseph Conger,[2] Adjutant.............. ———.......5-15-1778..McI.
183. Matthew McCalla,[2] First Lieutenant.... ———.......5-15-1778..McI.
184. William Faircloth,[2] First Lieutenant.... ———.......5-15-1778..McI.
185. Isaac Moore,[2] Captain,................. ———.......5-15-1778..McI.
186. James Wilson,[2] Captain................. ———.......5-15-1778..McI.
187. Silas Stevenson,[2] Captain............... ———.......5-15-1778..McI.
188. Demcy Gregory,[2] Captain............... ———.......5-15-1778..McI.
189. John Lowry,[2] Adjutant.................. ———.......5-15-1778..McI.
190. Thomas Shute,[2] Ensign.................. ———.......5-15-1778..McI.
191. John Richardson,[2] Ensign............... ———.......5——-1778..McI.
192. David Wright,[2] Ensign.................. ———.......5-15-1778..McI.
193. Levi Gatlin,[2] Ensign..................... ———.......5-12-1778..McI.
194. William Hargrave,[2] Ensign.............. ———.......5-12-1778..McI.
195. Richard Dickinson,[2] Lieutenant......... ———.......5-12-1778..McI.
196. John Murray,[1] Major....................VF.........5-28-1778..M.
197. Lewis Farmer,[1] Lieutenant Colonel......VF.........5-11-1778..M.
198. Walter Stewart,[1] Colonel................VF.........5-12-1778..M.
199. Joseph Finley,[1] Captain.................VF.........5-12-1778..M.

[1] From Pennsylvania.
[2] From North Carolina.

RECORDS OF THE WAR DEPARTMENT—VOL. 167

Number	Deponent	Office	Where taken	Date	Witness
200.	John Robb,[1]	Captain	VF	5-12-1778	M.
201.	Robert Gray,[1]	Captain	VF	5-12-1778	M.
202.	John Clark,[1]	Captain	VF	5-28-1778	M.
203.	John Nice,[1]	Captain	VF	5-11-1778	M.
204.	James Carnahan,[1]	Captain	VF	5-28-1778	M.
205.	James McMichael,[1]	First Lieutenant	VF	5-28-1778	M.
206.	George Gyger (Guyger),[1]	Lieutenant	VF	5-28-1778	M.
207.	James Bickham,[1]	Lieutenant	VF	5-28-1778	M.
208.	William McCrackan,[1]	Lieutenant	VF	5-12-1778	M.
209.	William Moore,[1]	Lieutenant	VF	5-13-1778	M.
210.	Samuel Kinney,	Lieutenant	VF	5-12-1778	M.
211.	John Parks,[1]	Lieutenant	VF	5-11-1778	M.
212.	John Gregg,[1]	Lieutenant	VF	5-12-1778	M.
213.	Joseph Brownlee,[1]	Lieutenant	VF	5-12-1778	M.
214.	Edward Speer (Spear),[1]	Ensign	VF	5-12-1778	M.
215.	William Johnson,[1]	Ensign	VF	5-12-1778	M.
216.	Joseph Gorman,[1]	Ensign	VF	5-24-1778	M.
217.	Joseph Collier,[1]	Ensign	Camp	5-12-1778	M.
218.	Jacob Weaver,[1]	Ensign	Camp	5-28-1778	M.
219.	Thomas Lincoln,[1]	Ensign	Camp	5-28-1778	M.
220.	Daniel Topham,	Lieutenant	Camp	5-28-1778	M.
221.	Andrew Little,[1]	Quarter Master	Camp	5-12-1778	M.
222.	Joseph Brown,[1]	Surgeon	Camp	5-12-1778	M.
223.	Aaron Woodruff,[1]	Surgeon's Mate	VF	5-11-1778	S.
224.	Nicholas Miller,[1]	Captain	VF	5-11-1778	S.
225.	Henry Makinly (McKinley),[1]	Captain	VF	5-11-1778	S.
226.	John Reily,[1]	Captain	VF	5-11-1778	S.
227.	Neigal Gray,[1]	Lieutenant Colonel	VF	5-11-1778	S.
228.	Andrew Ledlie,[1]	Surgeon	VF	5-11-1778	S.
229.	Thomas Dungan,[1]	Paymaster	VF	5-11-1778	S.
230.	Andrew Engel,[1]	Ensign	VF	5-11-1778	S.
231.	Stewart Herbert,[1]	Second Lieutenant	VF	5-11-1778	S.
232.	Stephen Chambers,[1]	Captain	VF	5-23-1778	S.
233.	George Vaughn,[1]	Quarter Master	VF	5-23-1778	S.
234.	Blackall William Ball,[1]	Lieutenant	VF	5-23-1778	S.
235.	John Boyd,[1]	Lieutenant	VF	6- 4-1778	S.
236.	Omitted.				
237.	Samuel Dawson,[1]	Captain	MJ	6- 4-1778	W.
238.	James Mackey,[1]	First Lieutenant	MJ	6- 4-1778	W.
239.	Nicholas White,[1]	Volunteer	MJ	5-12-1778	W.
240.	Lazarus Stow,[1]	Lieutenant	MJ	5-12-1778	W.
241.	Mayberry Tolly,[1]	Captain	MJ	5——1778	W.

[1] From Pennsylvania.

| Number | Deponent | Office | Where taken | Date | Witness |

242. Francis Mentges,[1] Major................MJ..........5-—-1778..W.
243. Robert McMordie,[1] Chaplain...........MJ..........5-18-1778..W.
244. Caleb North,[1] Lieutenant Colonel.......MJ..........5-12-1778..W.
245. Jacob Giles Hicks,[1] First Lieutenant.....MJ..........5-12-1778..W.
246. Jacob Fiss,[1] Lieutenant.................MJ..........5-12-1778..W.
247. "Attestation of the 10th Penna. Regiment taken by Gen. Wayne."
248. George Nagel,[1] Colonel.................MJ..........5-12-1778..W.
249. William Cox,[1] Captain..................MJ..........5-12-1778..W.
250. Robert Patton,[1] First Lieutenant........MJ..........5-12-1778..W.
251. Joseph Banks,[1] Ensign..................MJ..........5-12-1778..W.
252. Daniel Dennis,[1] Second Lieutenant......MJ..........5-12-1778..W.
253. Peter Drummond,[1] First Lieutenant.....MJ..........5-12-1778..W.
254. William Feltman,[1] First Lieutenant......Mt.Pleas.....5-12-1778..W.
255. David Schrack[1], Captain................MJ..........5-12-1778..W.
256. Jacob Stake,[1] Captain..................MJ..........5-12-1778..W.
257. Abraham Hargis,[1] First Lieutenant......MJ..........5-12-1778..W.
257½. George Calhoun,[1] Captain.............MJ..........5-12-1778..W.
258. Robert Hooper,[1] Second Lieutenant......MJ..........5-12-1778..W.
259. Alexander Benstead,[1] Paymaster........MJ..........5-12-1778..W.
260. Francis Adams,[1] First Lieutenant.......MJ..........5-12-1778..W.
261. James Grier,[1] Major....................MJ..........5-12-1778..W.
262. Harman Stout,[1] Captain................MJ..........5-12-1778..W.
263. Adam Keller,[1] Second Lieutenant........MJ..........5-12-1778..W.
264. William Knox,[1] First Lieutenant........MJ..........5-12-1778..W.
265. Adam Hubley,[1] Lieutenant Colonel......MJ..........5-12-1778..W.
266. James McLean,[1] Adjutant...............MJ..........5-12-1778..W.
267. John Steel,[1] First Lieutenant...........MJ..........5-22-1778..W.
268. John Cole,[1] Second Lieutenant..........MJ..........5-12-1778..W.
269. James Long,[1] Captain (Affirmation)......MJ..........5-12-1778..W.
270. William Magaw,[1] Surgeon...............VF..........5-11-1778..S.
271. Samuel Platt,[1] Surgeon's Mate..........VF..........5-11-1778..S.
272. Thomas Bartholomew Bowen[1], Captain...VF..........5-11-1778..S.
273. Jacob Vanderslice,[1] Lieutenant..........VF..........5-11-1778..S.
274. George Knox,[1] Quarter Master..........VF..........5-11-1778..S.
275. Samuel Davis,[1] Lieutenant..............VF..........5-11-1778..S.
276. Robert McBride,[1] Lieutenant............VF..........5-11-1778..S.
277. Joseph McClellan,[1] Captain..............VF..........5-11-1778..S.
278. Nicholas Coleman,[1] Lieutenant..........VF..........5-11-1778..S.
279. William Vanlear,[1] Lieutenant...........VF..........5-11-1778..S.
280. Francis Nichols,[1] Major.................VF..........5-11-1778..S.
281. John McKinney,[1] Ensign................VF..........5-11-1778..S.

[1] From Pennsylvania.

RECORDS OF THE WAR DEPARTMENT—VOL. 167 49

Number	Deponent Office	Where taken	Date	Witness
282.	Richard Butler,[1] Colonel	VF	5-11-1778	S.
283.	Daniel Darragh,[1] Lieutenant	VF	5-25-1778	S.
284.	John Birkman,[1] Lieutenant	VF	5-27-1778	S.
285.	William Thompson,[1] Adjutant	VF	5-30-1778	S.
286.	George Grant,[1] Captain	VF	5-28-1778	S.
287.	Thomas Swyler,[1] Ensign	VF	5-30-1778	S.
288.	John Ashton-, Lieutenant	VF	5-30-1778	S.
289.	John Tate,[1] Paymaster	VF	5-30-1778	S.
290.	John Davis,[1] Captain	VF	5-28-1778	S.
291.	Mordecai Morgan,[1] First Lieutenant	VF	5-28-1778	S.
292.	Matt: Henderson-, Captain	VF	5-30-1778	S.
293.	Frederic Vernon,[1] Major (Affirmation)	MJ	5-12-1778	W.
294.	John Crawford,[1] Adjutant	MJ	6- 2-1778	W.
295.	Stephen Bayard,[1] Lieutenant Colonel	MJ	5-12-1778	W.
296.	Daniel Brodhead,[1] Colonel	VF	5-12-1778	W.
297.	Benjamin Neilly,[1] First Lieutenant	MJ	5-12-1778	W.
298.	William Amberson,[1] Second Lieutenant	MJ	5-12-1778	W.
299.	John Finley,[1] Captain	MJ	5-12-1778	W.
300.	James Milligan,[1] Second Lieutenant	MJ	5-12-1778	W.
301.	John Blair,[1] Lieutenant	MJ	5-12-1778	W.
302.	Samuel Kennedy,[1] First Lieutenant	MJ	5-12-1778	W.
303.	William Irvine,[1] Colonel	MJ	5-12-1778	W.
304.	John Alexander,[1] Captain	MJ	5-12-1778	W.
305.	John Bush,[1] First Lieutenant	MJ	5-12-1778	W.
306.	Robert McPherson,[1] First Lieutenant	MJ	5-12-1778	W.
307.	James Williamson,[1] Second Lieutenant	MJ	5-12-1778	W.
308.	Andrew Irvine,[1] Captain	MJ	5—-1778	W.
309.	Joseph Torrans (Torrance),[1] Lieutenant	MJ	5-15-1778	W.
310.	William Lusk,[1] First Lieutenant	MJ	5—-1778	W.
311.	John Rose,[1] Surgeon	MJ	5-12-1778	W.
312.	Sam Montgomery,[1] Captain	MJ	5-19-1778	W.
313.	Robert Peebles,[1] Second Lieutenant	MJ	5-12-1778	W.
314.	John McCullam,[1] Second Lieutenant	MJ	5—-1778	W.
315.	Alexander Russel,[1] First Lieutenant	MJ	5—-1778	W.
316.	Samuel Hay,[1] Major	MJ	5-12-1778	W.
317.	John Hughes,[1] Second Lieutenant	MJ	5—-1778	W.
318.	Robert Blackwell,[1] Chaplain	MJ	5-30-1778	W.
319.	John Hughes,[1] Second Lieutenant	MJ	5-12-1778	W.

[1] From Pennsylvania.

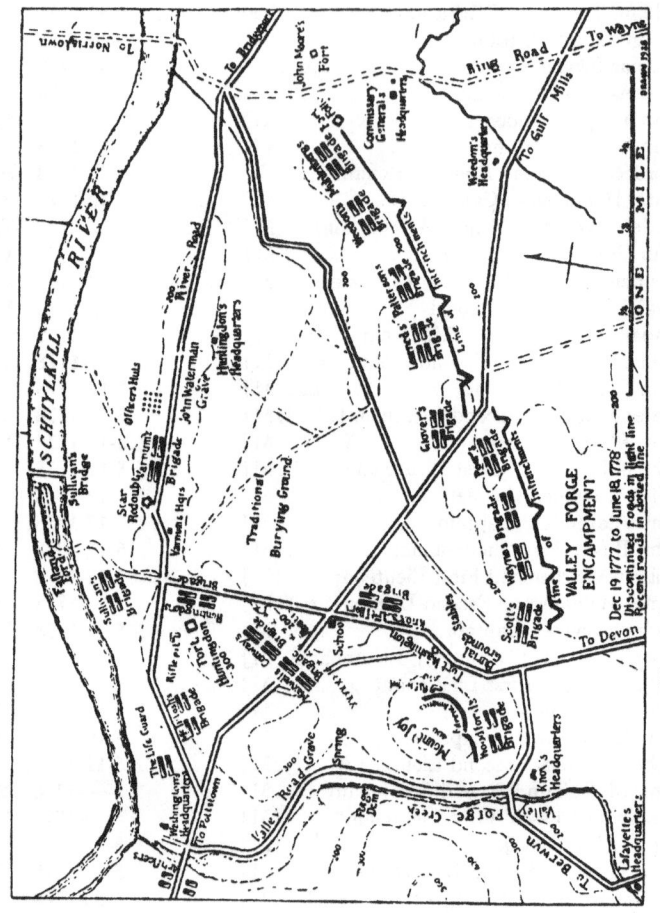

The original of this map is in the Library of Congress.

Volume 168

Records of the War Department

in

The National Archives

Number	Deponent	Office	Where taken	Date	Witness
320.	Andrew Johnston,	Quarter Master	MJ	5-12-1778	W.
321.	Edward Crawford,[1]	Third Lieutenant	MJ	5-12-1778	W.
322.	William McDowell,[1]	Third Lieutenant	MJ	5-12-1778	W.
323.	Robert Clifton,[1]	Third Lieutenant	MJ	5-12-1778	W.
324.	David Hamond,[1]	Third Lieutenant	MJ	5-12-1778	W.
325.	Aaron Norcross,[1]	Second Lieutenant	MJ	5-12-1778	W.
326.	Samuel Brady,[1]	First Lieutenant	MJ	5-12-1778	W.
327.	Benjamin Lyons,[1]	First Lieutenant	MJ	5-12-1778	W.
328.	David Ziegler,[1]	First Lieutenant	MJ	5-12-1778	W.
329.	Michael Ryan,	Major	MJ	5-12-1778	W.
330.	James Chambers,[1]	Colonel	MJ	5-12-1778	W.
331.	James Wilson,[1]	Captain	MJ	5-12-1778	W.
332.	John Doyle,[1]	Captain	MJ	5-12-1778	W.
333.	Samuel Craig,[1]	Captain	MJ	5-12-1778	W.
334.	Henry McCormick,[1]	Brigade Major	MJ	5-12-1778	W.
335.	Michael Simpson,[1]	Captain	MJ	5-12-1778	W.
336.	Thomas Doyle,[1]	Third Lieutenant	MJ	5-26-1778	W.
337.	James Mcfarland,[1]	Second Lieutenant	MJ	5-19-1778	W.
338.	George Jenkins,[1]	Captain	———	5-12-1778	W.
339.	James Moore,[1]	Major	MJ	5-12-1778	W.
340.	David Marshall,[1]	Second Lieutenant	MJ	5-12-1778	W.
341.	Persifor Frazer,[1]	Lieutenant Colonel	MJ	5-30-1778	W.
342.	Josiah Harmar,[1]	Lieutenant Colonel	VF	5-11-1778	S.
343.	Luke Brodhead,[1]	Captain	VF	5-11-1778	S.
344.	John McCowan,[1]	Captain	VF	5-11-1778	S.
345.	James Glentworth,[1]	Lieutenant	VF	5-11-1778	S.
346.	Charles Macnet,[1]	Ensign	VF	5-11-1778	S.
347.	Walter Cruize,[1]	Captain	VF	5-11-1778	S.
348.	James Waugh,[1]	Captain	VF	5-11-1778	S.
349.	Philip Snider,[1]	Ensign	VF	5-11-1778	S.
350.	Jeremiah Talbot,[1]	Major	VF	5-11-1778	S.
351.	John Savidge,[1]	Lieutenant	VF	5-11-1778	S.
352.	William Claypoole,[1]	Surgeon's Mate	VF	5-11-1778	S.
353.	John Foster,[1]	Ensign	VF	5-11-1778	S.
354.	Greenberry Hughes,[1]	Lieutenant	VF	5-11-1778	S.

[1] From Pennsylvania.

52 OATHS OF ALLEGIANCE

Number	Deponent	Office	Where taken	Date	Witness
355.	Farquher McPherson,[1]	Lieutenant	VF	5-27-1778	S.
356.	Jacob Bower,[1]	Captain	VF	5-27-1778	S.
357.	Enoch Morgan,[1]	Paymaster	VF	5-11-1778	S.
358.	John Markland,[1]	Ensign	VF	5-27-1778	S.
359.	Thomas Curtis,[2]	First Lieutenant	Camp	5-29-1778	M.
360.	William Baxter,[1]	Ensign	VF	5-27-1778	S.
361.	John Steel,[2]	Ensign	Camp	5-28-1778	M.
362.	William Pride,[2]	Lieutenant	Camp	5-12-1778	M.
363.	Nicholas Currell,[2]	Lieutenant	Camp	5-12-1778	M.
364.	Matthew Clay,[2]	Lieutenant	————	5-12-1778	M.
365.	Nathaniel G. Morris,[2]	Captain	————	5-11-1778	M.
366.	John Fitzgerald,[2]	Lieutenant	Camp	5-12-1778	M.
367.	Robert Beale,[2]	Lieutenant	Camp	5-12-1778	M.
368.	Lipscomb Norvell,[2]	Paymaster	Camp	5-12-1778	M.
369.	David Miller,[2]	Lieutenant	Camp	5-12-1778	M.
370.	Thomas Gaskins,[2]	Major	Camp	5-12-1778	M.
371.	Richard Kinnon,[2]	Lieutenant	Camp	5-12-1778	M.
372.	Andrew Russell,[2]	Captain	Camp	5-12-1778	M.
373.	William Fowler,[2]	Captain	Camp	5-12-1778	M.
374.	Edward Duff,[2]	Surgeon	Camp	5-11-1778	M.
375.	John Roney,[2]	Adjutant	Camp	5-12-1778	M.
376.	Samuel Colston,[2]	Captain	Camp	5-21-1778	M.
377.	John Anderson,[2]	Lieutenant	VF	5-25-1778	M.
378.	William Bentley,[2]	First Lieutenant	Camp	5-28-1778	M.
379.	John McAdam,[2]	Lieutenant	Camp	5-25-1778	M.
380.	Alexander Balmain,	Chaplain	Camp	5-28-1778	M.
381.	Nathaniel Anderson,[2]	Lieutenant	Camp	5-25-1778	M.
382.	Uriah Springer,[2]	Lieutenant	Camp	5-11-1778	M.
383.	John McKinley,[2]	Lieutenant	Camp	5-11-1778	M.
384.	Arthur Gordon,[2]	Lieutenant	Camp	5-11-1778	M.
385.	James Neale,[2]	Captain	Camp	5-11-1778	M.
386.	Anthony Roger (Riger),[2]	Ensign	Camp	5-11-1778	M.
387.	David Steel,[2]	Captain	Camp	5-11-1778	M.
388.	Robert Beall,[2]	Captain	Camp	5-11-1778	M.
389.	Thomas Moore,[2]	Lieutenant	————	5-11-1778	M.
390.	Lewis Thomas,[2]	Lieutenant	Camp	5-11-1778	M.
391.	Andrew Lewis,[2]	Ensign	Camp	5-11-1778	M.
392.	Daniel DeBenneville,	-Surgeon	Camp	5-11-1778	M.
393.	Richard Campbell,[2]	Major	Camp	5-25-1778	M.
394.	Nathan Lamb (Lamme),[2]	Lieutenant	Camp	5-11-1778	M.
395.	John Green,[2]	Colonel	Camp	5-12-1778	M.

[1] From Pennsylvania.
[2] From Virginia.

RECORDS OF THE WAR DEPARTMENT—VOL. 168

Number	Deponent	Office	Where taken	Date	Witness
396.	Thomas Hard,[2]	Lieutenant	Camp	5-12-1778	M.
397.	Archibald Alexander,[2]	Surgeon	Camp	5-12-1778	M.
398.	James Dillard,[2]	Lieutenant	Camp	5-12-1778	M.
399.	Joseph Blackwell,[2]	Lieutenant	Camp	5-12-1778	M.
400.	John Robertson,[2]	Adjutant	Camp	5-12-1778	M.
401.	James Williams,[2]	Lieutenant	Camp	5-12-1778	M.
402.	James Hamilton,[2]	Lieutenant	Camp	5-12-1778	M.
403.	Thomas Blackwell,[2]	Captain	Camp	5-12-1778	M.
404.	Samuel Baskerville,[2]	Lieutenant	Camp	5-12-1778	M.
405.	Thomas Fox,[2]	Lieutenant	Camp	5-12-1778	M.
406.	John Gillison,[2]	Captain	Camp	5-12-1778	M.
407.	Thomas Barbee,[2]	Lieutenant	Camp	5-12-1778	M.
408.	Thomas West,[2]	Captain	Camp	5-12-1778	M.
409.	John Mountjoy,[2]	Captain	Camp	5-11-1778	M.
410.	Machen Boswell,[2]	First Lieutenant	——	6- 1-1778	M.
411.	Clough Shetton,[2]	Captain	Camp	5-12-1778	M.
412.	John Flut (Fleet),[2]	Second Lieutenant	Camp	6- 1-1778	M.
413.	Thomas Armistead,[2]	Lieutenant	Camp	5-12-1778	M.
414.	Abner Crump,[2]	Captain	Camp	5-12-1778	M.
415.	John Piper,[2]	Lieutenant	Camp	5-12-1778	M.
416.	Wyatt Coleman,[2]	Lieutenant	Camp	5-12-1778	M.
417.	Thomas C. Hoomes,[2]	Lieutenant	Camp	5-12-1778	M.
418.	John Best,[2]	Lieutenant	Camp	5-12-1778	M.
419.	James Merriweather,[2]	Lieutenant	Camp	5-12-1778	M.
420.	Windsor Brown,[2]	Captain	Camp	5-12-1778	M.
421.	Epaphroditus Rudder,[2]	Lieutenant	Camp	5-12-1778	M.
422.	William Brent,[2]	Lieutenant Colonel	Camp	5-12-1778	M.
423.	John Allison,[2]	Major	Camp	5-12-1778	M.
424.	John Lee,[2]	Captain	Camp	5-12-1778	M.
425.	Thomas Ewell,[2]	Captain	Camp	5-12-1778	M.
426.	Thomas Hamilton,[2]	Captain	Camp	5-12-1778	M.
427.	William Campbell,[2]	Lieutenant	Camp	5-12-1778	M.
428.	George Triplett,[2]	Lieutenant	Camp	5-12-1778	M.
429.	Peter Stubblefield,[2]	Lieutenant	Camp	5-12-1778	M.
430.	John Nicholas,[2]	Captain	Camp	5-11-1778	M.
431.	Thomas Merriweather,[2]	Captain	Camp	5-11-1778	M.
432.	Frederick Woodson,	Lieutenant	Camp	5-11-1778	M.
433.	John Cole,[2]	Second Lieutenant	Camp	5-12-1778	M.
434.	Thomas Parker,[2]	Lieutenant	Camp	5-12-1778	M.
435.	Francis Cowherd,[2]	Lieutenant	Camp	5-12-1778	M.
436.	John Crawford,[2]	Lieutenant	Camp	5-12-1778	M.
437.	Thomas Catlett,[2]	Lieutenant	Camp	5-12-1778	M.

[2] From Virginia.

Number	Deponent	Office	Where taken	Date	Witness

438. Rhodam Mocksly,[3] Quarter Master......Camp........5-12-1778..M.
439. Benjamin Hoomes,[2] Captain............Camp........5-12-1778..M.
440. William Porter,[2] Ensign...............Camp........5-12-1778..M.
441. Marcus Calmes,[2] Captain..............Camp........5-12-1778..M.
442. John Kennon,[2] Lieutenant.............Camp........5-12-1778..M.
443. Alexander Parker,[2] Captain............Camp........5-12-1778..M.
444. Samuel Cobbs,[2] Lieutenant............Camp........5-12-1778..M.
445. Rudolph Falkner,[2] Major..............Camp........5-12-1778..M.
446. Christian Febiger,[2] Colonel...........Camp........5-11-1778..M.
447. James Moody,[2] Lieutenant............,...Camp........6- 1-1778..M.
448. Nathaniel Welch,[2] Second Lieutenant....————......6- 8-1778..M.
449. Benj. C. Spiller,[2] Captain..............————......5-25-1778..M.
450. John Baytop,[2] Ensign..................Camp........6- 1-1778..M.
451. Thomas Quarles,[2] Ensign...............Camp........6- 8-1778..M.
452. William Evans,[2] Lieutenant............Camp........5-12-1778..M.
453. John Harkley,[2] Ensign.................Camp........5-12-1778..M.
454. William Stirling Smith,[2] Quarter Master..Camp........5-12-1778..M.
455. Charles Simms,[2] Lieutenant Colonel......Camp........5-12-1778..M.
456. John Roberts,[2] Surgeon.................Camp........5-12-1778..M.
457. Richard Apperson,[2] Captain............Camp........5-12-1778..M.
458. Simon Summers,[2] Adjutant.............Camp........5-12-1778..M.
459. James Mabon,[2] Lieutenant..............Camp........5-12-1778..M.
459½. James Quarles,[2] Captain...............Camp........6- 8-1778..M.
460. William Hudson,[2] Lieutenant...........Camp........5-12-1778..M.
461. John Gibson,[2] Colonel..................Camp........5-12-1778..M.
462. John Stokes,[2] Lieutenant...............Camp........5-12-1778..M.
463. Austin Sandridge,[2] Quarter Master.......Camp........5-12-1778..M.
464. Thomas Massie,[2] Captain...............Camp........5- 2-1778..M.
465. James Barnett,[2] Lieutenant.............Camp........5-28-1778..M.
466. Samuel Hopkins,[2] Major................Camp........5-28-1778..M.
467. John Kinnon,[2] Paymaster...............Camp........5-28-1778..M.
468. Jacob Snider,[1] Lieutenant...............Camp........7-27-1778..W.
469. John Bankson,[1] Captain.................Camp........7-21-1778..W.
470. Christian Staddle,[1] Captain.............————......5——-1778..W.
471. Henry Piercy,[1] First Lieutenant.........————......7-27-1778..W.
472. Abel Morris,[1] Lieutenant...............Rdg..........2——-1778..—.
473. James Johnston,[1] First Lieutenant & Paymaster................................————......5-12-1778..W.
474. William McMurray,[1] Second Lieutenant..MJ..........5-26-1778..W.
475. William Williams,[1] Major...............————......5-28-1778..?

[1] From Pennsylvania.
[2] From Virginia.
[3] Not Signed.

Number	Deponent Office	Where taken	Date	Witness
476.	John Stoy,[1] First Lieutenant	———	6- 4-1778	W.
477.	Jacob Ashmead,[1] Captain	———	6- 4-1778	W.
478.	Henry Bicker,[1] Colonel	———	5-12-1778	W.
479.	Thomas Craig,[1] Colonel	VF	5-11-1778	S.
480.	Rudolph Bunner,[1] Lieutenant Colonel	VF	5-11-1778	S.
481.	Peter Smith,[1] Quarter Master	VF	5-11-1778	S.
482.	Percival Butler,[1] Lieutenant	VF	5-11-1778	S.
483.	John Marshall,[1] First Lieutenant	VF	5-11-1778	S.
484.	James Tate,[1] Surgeon	VF	5-11-1778	S.
485.	John Wigton,[1] Paymaster	VF	5-11-1778	S.
486.	George McCully,[1] Lieutenant	VF	5-11-1778	S.
487.	Thomas L. Moore,[1] Captain	VF	5-25-1778	S.
488.	Thomas Butler,[1] Captain	VF	5-11-1778	S.
489.	James Chrystie,[1] Captain	VF	5-23-1778	S.
490.	John Huling,[1] Major	VF	5-23-1778	S.
491.	James Black,[1] Lieutenant	VF	5-11-1778	S.
492.	James Armstrong,[1] First Lieutenant	VF	5-27-1778	S.
493.	James Jones,[1] Surgeon's Mate	MJ	5-12-1778	W.
494.	Ben. Fishbourn,[1] Captain	MJ	5-12-1778	W.
495.	Thomas Church,[1] Major	MJ	5-12-1778	W.
496.	William Butler,[1] Lieutenant Colonel	MJ	5-12-1778	W.
497.	David Jones,[1] Chaplain	MJ	5-12-1778	W.
498.	David Brown,[1] Lieutenant	MJ	5-12-1778	W.
499.	E. Beatty,[1] Lieutenant	MJ	5-12-1778	W.
500.	William Henderson,[1] Lieutenant	MJ	5-12-1778	W.
501.	Edward F. Randolph,[1] Lieutenant	MJ	5-12-1778	W.
502.	Benjamin Burd,[1] Captain	MJ	5-12-1778	W.
503.	Richard Allison,[1] Surgeon's Mate	MJ	5-12-1778	W.
504.	Jonathan Pugh,[1] Second Lieutenant	MJ	5-12-1778	W.
505.	Thomas Boude,[1] Captain	MJ	5-12-1778	W.
506.	Peter Summers,[1] Lieutenant	MJ	5-15-1778	W.
507.	Isaac Tuly,[1] Captain	MJ	5-12-1778	W.
508.	Michael Kimmell,[1] Paymaster	MJ	5-12-1778	W.
509.	John Bartley, First Lieutenant	MJ	5-12-1778	W.
510.	John Christy,[1] Captain	MJ	5-12-1778	W.
511.	Samuel Smith,[1] Captain	MJ	5-12-1778	W.
512.	Robert Gregg,[1] Captain	MJ	5-12-1778	W.
513.	Francis Johnston,[1] Colonel	MJ	5-12-1778	W.
514.	Abraham Wood,[1] Second Lieutenant	MJ	5-12-1778	W.
515.	George North,[1] First Lieutenant	MJ	5-12-1778	W.
516.	Benjamin Bartholomew,[1] Captain	MJ	5-12-1778	W.
517.	William Schofield,[1] First Lieutenant	MJ	5-12-1778	W.

[1] From Pennsylvania.

56 OATHS OF ALLEGIANCE

Number	Deponent	Office	Where taken	Date	Witness
518.	Job Vernon,[1]	First Lieutenant	MJ	5-12-1778	W.
519.	James Davidson,[1]	Surgeon	——	5-28-1778	W.
520.	Alexander Rose,[2]	Captain	Camp	5-28-1778	M.
521.	Beverly Stubblefield,[2]	Lieutenant	Camp	5-28-1778	M.
522.	Richard Taylor,[2]	Lieutenant	Camp	5-28-1778	M.
523.	Edmund B. Dickinson,[2]	Major	Camp	5-12-1778	M.
524.	Callohill Minnis,[2]	Captain	Camp	(torn)-1778	M.
525.	Benjamin Green,	Paymaster	VF	5-30-1778	M.
526.	Thomas Pemberton,	Lieutenant	——	5——-1778	M.
527.	Thomas Holt,[2]	Lieutenant	Camp	5-28-1778	—.
528.	William Cunningham,[2]	Captain	Camp	5-28-1778	M.
529.	Charles Yarbrough,[2]	Lieutenant	——	6——-1778	M.
530.	Joseph Selden,[2]	First Lieutenant	——	6- 1-1778	M.
531.	Jacob Valentine,[2]	Captain	Camp	5-29-1778	M.
532.	Charles Russell,[2]	Lieutenant	——	6- 4-1778	—.
533.	Richard Parker,[2]	Colonel	Camp	5-11-1778	M.
534.	John Drewry (Drury),[2]	Lieutenant	Camp	5-11-1778	M.
535.	Joseph Scott,[2]	Lieutenant	Camp	5-11-1778	M.
536.	Charles Pelham,[2]	Captain	Camp	5-11-1778	M.
537.	Thomas Bowne,[2]	Lieutenant	Camp	5-11-1778	M.
538.	Francis Minnis,[2]	Lieutenant	Camp	5-11-1778	M.
539.	Ballard Smith,[2]	Lieutenant	Camp	5-11-1778	M.
540.	Alexander Dickey,[2]	Muster Master	Camp	5-11-1778	M.
541.	Alexander Skinner,[2]	Surgeon	——	5-11-1778	M.
542.	Marks Vanderwall,[2]	Lieutenant	——	5-11-1778	M.
543.	Samuel Selden,[2]	Lieutenant	Camp	5-11-1778	M.
544.	Claiborne W. Lawson,[2]	Captain	Camp	5-11-1778	M.
545.	John Sutton,[2]	Paymaster	Camp	5-11-1778	M.
546.	William Pointer,[2]	Second Lieutenant	Camp	5-11-1778	M.
547.	John Marks,[2]	Captain	Camp	5-28-1778	M.
548.	Richard Claiborne,	Brigade Major	VF	5-28-1778	M.
549.	Richard Worsham,[2]	Second Lieutenant	Camp	5-14-1778	M.
550.	Burwell Green,[2]	Ensign	Camp	5-28-1778	M.
551.	John Overton,[2]	Captain	Camp	5-14-1778	M.
552.	Joseph Conway,[2]	Ensign	Camp	5-18-1778	M.
553.	William Tucker,[2]	Second Lieutenant	Camp	5-14-1778	M.
554.	Abraham Buford,[2]	Lieutenant Colonel	Camp	5-28-1778	M.
555.	Abraham Maury, Jr.,[2]	Lieutenant	Camp	5-29-1778	M.
556.	David Merriweather,[2]	Lieutenant	Camp	5-29-1778	M.
557.	Nathaniel Terry,[2]	Lieutenant	Camp	5-11-1778	M.
558.	Samuel I. Cabell,[2]	Major	Camp	5-11-1778	M.

[1] From Pennsylvania.
[2] From Virginia.

RECORDS OF THE WAR DEPARTMENT—VOL. 168

Number	Deponent Office	Where taken	Date	Witness
559.	John Spencer,[2] Surgeon	Camp	--29-1778	M.
560.	John B. Johnson,[2] Lieutenant	Camp	5-28-1778	M.
561.	William Eppes,[2] Lieutenant	Camp	5-28-1778	M.
562.	William Jenkins,[2] Lieutenant	Camp	5-12-1778	M.
563.	Drury Oliver,[2] Lieutenant	———	5-11-1778	M.
564.	Syrus (Cyrus) L. Roberts,[2] Captain	Camp	5-12-1778	M.
565.	Peter Jones,[2] Captain	Camp	5-12-1778	M.
566.	David Walker,[2] Lieutenant	Camp	5-12-1778	M.
567.	William Davies,[2] Colonel	Camp	5-12-1778	M.
568.	Jacob Moon,[2] Paymaster	Camp	5-12-1778	M.
569.	Thomas Holt,[2] First Lieutenant	Camp	5-12-1778	M.
570.	George Holland,[2] First Lieutenant	Camp	5-12-1778	M.
571.	Samuel Campbell,[2] First Lieutenant	Camp	5-12-1778	M.
572.	Nathan Reid,[2] Captain	Camp	5-12-1778	M.
573.	Peter Davie,[3] Quarter Master	Camp	5-12-1778	M.
574.	Thomas Burfoot,[2] Adjutant	Camp	5-12-1778	M.
575.	Alexander Ewing,[2] First Lieutenant	Camp	5-12-1778	M.
576.	John Dudley,[2] First Lieutenant	Camp	5-12-1778	M.
577.	John McElheany,[2] Second Lieutenant	Camp	5-18-1778	M.
578.	Bartlet Collins,[2] Ensign	Camp	5-18-1778	M.
579.	H. Dudley,[2] Captain	Camp	5-18-1778	M.
580.	Thomas Bressie,[2] Captain	Camp	5-18-1778	M.
581.	Lodowick Brodie (Broady), Surgeon's Mate	Camp	5-18-1778	M.
582.	Gregory Smith,[2] Colonel	Camp	5-18-1778	M.
583.	William Long,[2] First Lieutenant	Camp	5-18-1778	M.
584.	Levin Walker,[2] Ensign	Camp	5-18-1778	M.
585.	John Worsham,[2] Lieutenant	Camp	5-18-1778	M.
586.	Benjamin Biggs,[2] First Lieutenant	Camp	5-18-1778	M.
587.	Thomas Parramore,[2] Captain	Camp	5-18-1778	M.
588.	Thomas Clark,[2] First Lieutenant	Camp	5-18-1778	M.
589.	Samuel Waples,[2] First Lieutenant	Camp	5-18-1778	M.
590.	John Machenheimer,[4] Ensign	Camp	5-18-1778	M.
591.	Henry Fauntleroy,[2] Captain	Camp	5-18-1778	M.
592.	Thomas Overton,[2] Second Lieutenant	Camp	5-18-1778	M.
593.	Burges Ball,[2] Lieutenant Colonel	Camp	5-18-1778	M.
594.	Robert H. Saunders,[2] Lieutenant	Camp	5-18-1778	M.
595.	Claiborne Vaughn,[2] Surgeon's Mate	Camp	5-18-1778	M.
596.	Robert Ballard,[2] Lieutenant Colonel	Camp	5-18-1778	M.
597.	William Lewis,[2] Captain	Camp	5-18-1778	M.

[2] From Virginia.
[3] Not Signed.
[4] German Battalion.

58   OATHS OF ALLEGIANCE

Number	Deponent Office	Where taken	Date	Witness
598.	John D. Woelper,[4] Captain	Camp	5-18-1778	M.
599.	George Hubley,[4] Captain	Camp	5-18-1778	M.
600.	Holman Mennis,[2] Lieutenant	Camp	5-18-1778	M.
601.	Tarlton Payne,[2] Captain	Camp	5-18-1778	M.
602.	Miles King,[2] Surgeon's mate	Camp	5-18-1778	M.
603.	John Harrison,[2] Ensign	Camp	5-18-1778	M.
604.	Samuel Hogg,[2] Lieutenant	Camp	5-18-1778	M.
605.	Peter Boyer,[4] Captain	Camp	5-18-1778	M.
606.	David Allen,[2] Ensign	Camp	5-18-1778	M.
607.	William Rice,[4] Lieutenant	Camp	5-18-1778	M.
608.	Lodowick Wirtenberg,[4] Surgeon	Camp	5-18-1778	M.
609.	George Cole,[4] Ensign	Camp	5-18-1778	M.
610.	John Weidman,[4] Lieutenant	Camp	5-18-1778	M.
611.	Richard C. Anderson,[2] Captain	Camp	5-18-1778	M.
612.	John Stricker,[1] Second Lieutenant	——	5-12-1778	W.
613.	James Morris Jones,[1] Second Lieutenant	——	5-12-1778	W.
614.	William Litzsinger,[4] Ensign	Camp	5-18-1778	M.
615.	Charles Darragh,[1] Second Lieutenant	——	5-12-1778	W.
616.	Samuel Tolbert,[1] Captain	——	5-12-1778	W.
617.	Henry D. Pursell,[1] Second Lieutenant	——	5-12-1778	W.
618.	Thomas Norton,[1] Second Lieutenant	——	5-12-1778	W.
619.	John Irwin,[1] Adjutant	——	5-12-1778	W.
620.	Frederick Paschke, Captain & Quarter Master	——	10- 8-1778	M.
621.	John Brahan,* Lieutenant	"City of Washington"	3-25-1781	C.

* The editor feels obliged to make some remark concerning this Oath (No. 621, Vol. 168) because it is so evidently out of place in this collection. It is on a form printed for use in the first decade of the nineteenth century as is shown by the unfinished year date 180—. Notwithstanding this fact the person who filled in the Oath wrote the date "March the twenty-fifth seventeen hundred and eight-one," completely ignoring the printed form. Then there is "The City of Washington," another impossible anachronism if Washington, D. C. is meant. The only possible explanation of these discrepencies seems to be that the person who filled in the oath had a mental lapse. This supposition is supported by the notice of John Brahan in Heitman's Register. q.v.

[1] From Pennsylvania.
[4] German Battalion.

I, *Joshua Davis*, do acknowledge the United States of *America* to be free, Independent and sovereign States, and declare that the People thereof owe no Allegiance to *George* the Third, King of *Great-Britain*; and I renounce, refuse and abjure any Allegiance or Obedience to him; and I do swear that I will, to the Utmost of my Power, support, maintain and defend the said United States, against the said King *George* the Third, his Heirs and Successors, and his and their Abettors, Assistants and Adherents, and will serve the said United States in the Office of *Deputy Barrack Master Gen'l* which I now hold, with Fidelity, according to the best of my Skill and Understanding. So help me God. *Joshua Davis*

I, *Joshua Davis*, do swear that I will faithfully, truly and impartially execute the Office of *D'y Bar'k Master Gen'l* to which I am appointed, and render a true Account, when thereunto required, of all public Monies by me received or expended, and of all Stores or other Effects to me intrusted, which belong to the United States, and will, in all respects, discharge the Trust reposed in me with Justice and Integrity, to the best of my Skill and Understanding.
So help me God. *Josh'o Davis*

Head-Quarters, *Boston Mar. 6, 1778*
PERSONALLY appeared *Joshua Davis Esq'r Deputy Barrack Master Gen'l Eastern Department* and took the above Oaths by him subscribed.
Before me,
W. Heath M.G.

This item is interesting as it shows the Oath of Allegiance, the Oath of Fidelity in Office and the Certificate of Joshua Davis, all on one piece of paper.

Library of Congress Collection

of

Oaths of Allegiance

LIBRARY OF CONGRESS COLLECTION

ABBREVIATIONS

A.H.—A. C. Hansom
B.—Boston
Brm.—John Broom, Alderman of New York
B.P.—Benjamin Paschall, Justice of the Peace of Philadelphia
Cc.Pa.—Cumberland County, Pa.
C.G.—Cyrus Griffin
Cln.—Charlestown
Csl.—Carlisle, Pa.
C.T.—Charles Thomson
D.—James Davis, Justice of the Peace of North Carolina
E.B.—Elias Bourdinot
E.H.—Edward Hand
E.R.—Edmund Randolph
FK.—Fish Kill
G.B.—George Bryan, Justice of the Supreme Court of Pennsylvania
FP.—Fort Pitt
H.—William Heath
Hk.—John Hancock
H.L.—Henry Laurens
I.P.—Israel Putnam
I.S.—Isaac Smith, Justice of the Supreme Court of New Jersey
J.A.—John Avery
J.B.—Jonathan Brown, Justice of the Peace, Watertown
J.Bru.—John Bruchman, Justice of the Peace, South Carolina
J.C.—John Creigh, Justice of the Peace, Carlisle, Pa.
J.D.—James Duane, Mayor of New York
J.G.—John Gibson
J.H.—John Hanson

J.J.—John Jay
J.S.H.—John Slow Hobart
J.Y.—James Young
K.—Henry Knox
L.—Lancaster
M.—Peter Muhlenberg
McD.—Alexander McDougall
McI.—Lachlan McIntosh
M.W.—Mescech Weare, Chief Justice of New Hampshire
N.H.—New Hampshire
P.F.—Plunkett Fleeson
Ph.—Philadelphia
Rdg.—Reading
Rk.—Rockingham, N. H.
R.M.—Robert Morris
R.V.—Richard Varick
Sf.—Springfield (Mass.)
S.H.—Samuel Huntington
S.N.—Samuel Niles, Justice of the Peace of Boston
S.P.—Samuel Penhallon
St.C.—Arthur St.Clair
T.M.—Thomas Mifflin
T.McK.—Thomas McKean, Chief Justice of Pennsylvania.
W.A.—William Adcock
Wbg.—Williamsburg (Va.)
W.H.—William Henry, Justice of the Peace, Lancaster, Pa.
W.I.—William Irvine
W.N.—W. Neilson, Alderman of New York
Wt.—Watertown
Y.T.—York Town (York, Pa.)

I do solemnly Declare & affirm that I do not hold myself Bound to Bear faith & alegiance to George the 3.d King of Great Brittain I will

I Do solemnly Declare & affirm that I Do Bear faith & true alegiance to the united States of america & I will Do all in my Power to support the Laws established under the authority of the People I will

head Quarters Little Egg harbour   Adam Pittit
October 21. 1778   + IJ Silas Ireland
      Em Cajah Willbes
    + Stephen Ryers
    Noah Redgwa
    + Joseph Barber
    +a Samuel Parker
    + Joseph King
    + Peter Parker
    + Edward Parker
    James X Cramer
      Mark

Affirmation of Allegiance of a group of Quakers at Little Egg Harbor.

LIBRARY OF CONGRESS
COLLECTION

Page	Deponent Office	Where taken	Date	Witness
1.	John Dunlap, Printer	—	7-13-1776	J.G.
1.	D. C. Claypoole, Printer	—	7-13-1776	J.G.
2.	John Benezet, Commissioner of Claims	Ph	6-30-1777	Hk.
2.	Thomas Fitzsimmons, Commissioner of Claims	Ph	6-30-1777	Hk.
2.	Robert Richie, Commissioner of Claims	Ph	6-30-1777	Hk.
3.	Belcher P. Smith, Clerk in the Office of the Secretary of Congress	—	6-30-1777	Hk.
4.	Same as No. 3.			
5.	Jacob Rush, Deputy Secretary	—	11-10-1777	H.L.
6.	John Thaxter, Clerk in the Office of the Secretary of Congress	—	2-21-1778	H.L.
7.	John Benezet, Commissioner of Claims	Y.T.	2-21-1778	T.McK.
8.	Mark Bird, Colonel and Q.M.G.	Rdg	2-21-1778	T.M.
9.	John Gibson, Auditor General	Y.T.	2-21-1778	T.McK.
10.	William Govett,* Assistant Auditor General	Y.T.	2-21-1778	T.McK.
11.	Michael Hillegas, Continental Treasurer	Y.T.	2-21-1778	T.McK.
12.	Francis Hopkinson, Commissioner of the Navy Board	Y.T.	2-21-1778	T.McK.
13.	James Milligan, Commissioner of Claims	Y.T.	2-21-1778	T.McK.
14.	Thomas Peters, Commissioner of Prisoners	Y.T.	2-21-1778	T.McK.
15.	William Shippen, Jr., Director General of Hospitals of the United States	Rdg	2-21-1778	T.McK.
16.	Anthony Butler, Agent for Camp Equipage	Rdg	2-23-1778	T.M.
17.	Horatio Gates, Major General & President of the Board of War and Ordnance	Y.T.	2-23-1778	T.McK.
18.	Jacob Fitzsimmons, Agent for the Purchase of Horses, Waggons &c	Rdg	2-23-1778	T.M.
19.	Joseph Nourse, Secretary of Ordnance & Paymaster of the Board of War	Y.T.	2-23-1778	T.McK.
20.	John Ord, Justice of the Peace of Philadelphia & Manager of the Lottery of the United States	—	2-23-1778	J.Y.
21.	Richard Peters, Member of the Board of War & Ordnance	Y.T.	2-23-1778	T.McK.

* Affirmation.

LIBRARY OF CONGRESS COLLECTION 65

Page	Deponent Office	Where taken	Date	Witness
22.	Timothy Pickering	Y.T.	2-23-1778	T.McK.
23.	John Thaxter, Jr., Clerk to the Secretary of Congress	Y.T.	2-23-1778	T.McK.
24.	Daniel Oldenburch, Captain & Barrack at Lebanon	———	2-24-1778	M.
25.	Matthias Primer, Assistant Barrack Master at Lebanon	———	2-24-1778	M.
26.	Moses Hays, Assistant Deputy Q.M.G.	Rdg	2-26-1778	T.M.
27.	Henry Latimer, Senior Surgeon	Rdg	2-26-1778	T.M.
28.	Robert McDonald, Forage Master	Rdg	2-26-1778	T.M.
29.	Isaac Melcher, Colonel & Barrack Master General	Rdg	2-26-1778	T.M.
30.	Cornelius Sweers, Deputy Commissary General of Military Stores	———	2-26-1778	T.McK.
31.	John White, "An Express"	Rdg	2-26-1778	T.M.
31½.	George Nelson (Neilson), Clerk to the Q.M.G.	Rdg	2-28-1778	T.M.
32.	Frederick Phile, Senior Surgeon	———	3- 1-1778	W.H.
33.	Philetus Cumbersome, Express Rider	Rdg	3- 2-1778	T.M.
34.	Charles Souder, Captain of Artificers	Rdg	3- 2-1778	T.M.
35.	John Greaton, Colonel	B	3- 3-1778	H.
36.	Richard Gridley, Chief Engineer	B	3- 3-1778	H.
37.	William Heath, Major General	B	3- 3-1778	I.P.
38.	Israel Keith, Deputy Adjutant General	B	3- 3-1778	H.
39.	Seth Loring, Secretary to Major General Heath	B	3- 3-1778	H.
40.	Jonathan Pollard, Aid-de-Camp	B	3- 3-1778	H.
41.	Nathaniel Barber, Jr., Deputy Commissary of Military Stores	B	3- 4-1778	H.
42.	Andrew Brown, Deputy Muster Master	B	3- 4-1778	H.
43.	Henry Dearborn, Lieutenant Colonel	B	3- 4-1778	H.
44.	Henry Jackson, Colonel	B	3- 4-1778	H.
45.	Samuel Mellish, Quarter Master	B	3- 4-1778	H.
46.	John Callender, Captain Lieutenant of Artillery	B	3- 5-1778	H.
47.	Thomas Chace, Deputy Q.M.G.	B	3- 5-1778	H.
48.	Alexander Church, Assistant to the Q.M.G.	Rdg	3- 5-1778	T.M.
49.	Zaccheus Donnell, Lieutenant	B	3- 5-1778	H.
50.	Ebenezer Hancock, Deputy Paymaster General	B	3- 5-1778	H.
51.	William Hiltzheimer, Store Keeper	Rdg	3- 5-1778	T.M.
52.	Richard Hunnewell, Lieutenant	B	3- 5-1778	H.

66   OATHS OF ALLEGIANCE

Page	Deponent Office	Where taken	Date	Witness
53.	John Langdon, Captain	B	3- 5-1778	H.
54.	Thomas Smart, Pay Master	B	3- 5-1778	H.
55.	William Turnbull, Commissioner of Claims	Y.T	3- 5-1778	T.McK.
56.	Edward Archbald, Captain Lieutenant	B	3- 6-1778	H.
57.	Thomas Hollis Condy, Lieutenant	B	3- 6-1778	H.
58.	Michael Connolly, Lieutenant	B	3- 6-1778	H.
59.	Joshua Davis, Deputy Barrack Master General	B	3- 6-1778	H.
60.	Joseph Dunckerly, Adjutant	B	3- 6-1778	H.
61.	Aaron Haynes, Captain	B	3- 6-1778	H.
62.	John Hastings, Captain	B	3- 6-1778	H.
63.	David Hopkins, Captain	B	3- 6-1778	H.
64.	Matt: Irwin, Senior Surgeon	Rdg	3- 6-1778	T.M.
65.	Henry Knox, Brigadier General	B	3- 6-1778	H.
66.	Ezra Lunt, Captain	B	3- 6-1778	H.
67.	Samuel McKinsily (McKinzie), Senior Surgeon	Rdg	3- 6-1778	T.M.
68.	Daniel McLane, Lieutenant	B	3- 6-1778	H.
69.	Elisha Painter, Major of Artificers	B	3- 6-1778	H.
70.	Stephen Parker, Paymaster	B	3- 6-1778	H.
71.	Thomas Randall, Captain	B	3- 6-1778	H.
72.	Thomas Fosdick, Major	B	3- 6-1778	H.
73.	David Townsend, Senior Surgeon	B	3- 6-1778	H.
74.	John Warren, Senior Surgeon	B	3- 6-1778	H.
75.	Robert Williams, Paymaster	B	3- 6-1778	H.
76.	John Winston, Captain	B	3- 6-1778	H.
77.	Thomas Barker, Quarter Master	B	3- 7-1778	H.
78.	Dudley Colman, Lieutenant Colonel	B	3- 7-1778	H.
79.	Thomas Biggs, Clerk in Col. Flowers' Company	Cc.Pa	—-——	J.C.
80.	William Dawes, Lieutenant	B	3- 7-1778	H.
81.	Henry Haskell, Lieutenant Colonel	B	3- 7-1778	H.
82.	Bartlet Hindes, Lieutenant	B	3- 7-1778	H.
83.	Samuel Newman, Lieutenant	B	3- 7-1778	H.
84.	Amasa Soper, Captain	B	3- 7-1778	H.
85.	Benjamin Wallcutt, Captain	B	3- 7-1778	H.
86.	Samuel Whitwell, Jr., Surgeon	B	3- 7-1778	H.
87.	Jeduthan Baldwin, Engineer & Colonel	B	3- 9-1778	H.
88.	Thomas J. Carnes, Captain Lieutenant	B	3- 9-1778	H.
89.	Peter M. Crequi, Lieutenant	B	3- 9-1778	H.
90.	John Crosher, Lieutenant	B	3- 9-1778	H.
91.	William Lithgow, Major	B	3- 9-1778	H.

Library of Congress Collection 67

Page	Deponent Office	Where taken	Date	Witness
92.	William Courtis, Major	B	3-10-1778	H.
93.	William Mills, Lieutenant	B	3-10-1778	H.
94.	James Richardson, Assistant Commissary of Issues	B	3-10-1778	J.A.
95.	Joseph Scull, Clerk of Military Stores, Cumberland County, Pennsylvania.... ———		3-11-1778	J.C.
96.	Benjamin Eustis, Captain	B	3-11-1778	H.
97.	John Lillie, Captain	B	3-11-1778	H.
98.	William Story, Lieutenant	B	3-11-1778	H.
99.	Richard Bache, Post Master General of North America	L	3-20-1778	W.H.
100.	Richard Bache, Post Master General of North America	———	———————	W.H.
101.	Seth Bannister, Major	B	3-12-1778	H.
102.	George Dunham, Captain	B	3-12-1778	H.
103.	Jasper Ewing, Major	FP	3-12-1778	E.H.
104.	William Fenno, Quarter Master	B	3-22-1778	H.
105.	Benjamin Frothingham, Captain	B	3-12-1778	H.
106.	Richard Frothingham, Conductor of Ordnance Stores	B	3-12-1778	H.
107.	William Hunt, Assistant Commissary of Issues	Wt	3-12-1778	J.B.
108.	John Langdon, Agent for the Continent	Rk	3-12-1778	S.P.
109.	Ebenezer Learned, Brigadier General	B	3-12-1778	H.
110.	Daniel Loring, Assistant Commissary of Issues	B	3-12-1778	S.N.
111.	Samuel Shaw, Major	B	3-12-1778	H.
112.	Ezra Bodlam, Lieutenant Colonel	B	3-14-1778	H.
113.	Robert Bradford, Quarter Master	B	3-14-1778	H.
114.	Robert Davis, Captain	B	3-14-1778	H.
115.	Abraham Hunt, Captain	B	3-14-1778	H.
116.	Hez'h Ripley, Lieutenant	B	3-14-1778	H.
117.	John Thomas, Surgeon	B	3-14-1778	H.
118.	Joseph Thomas, Captain	B	3-14-1778	H.
119.	James Wesson, Colonel	B	3-14-1778	H.
120.	Thomas Burkman, Lieutenant	B	3-17-1778	H.
121.	Isaiah Bussey, Captain Lieutenant	B	3-17-1778	H.
122.	Nathaniel Cushing, Captain	B	3-17-1778	H.
123.	Thomas Dean, Captain Lieutenant	B	3-17-1778	H.
124.	Alexander Orr, Lieutenant	B	3-17-1778	H.
125.	John Popkins, Lieutenant Colonel	B	3-17-1778	H.
126.	William Stevens, Captain Lieutenant	B	3-17-1778	H.
127.	Samuel Cogswell, Lieutenant	B	3-18-1778	H.

68   OATHS OF ALLEGIANCE

Page   Deponent   Office   Where taken   Date   Witness
128. Samuel Sarjant, Superintendent and Keeper
     of Stores in Cumberland County, Pennsylvania...........................Csl..........3-18-1778..J.C.
129. Joseph Crocker, Paymaster.............B...........3-18-1778..H.
130. Daniel Lyman, Captain.................B...........3-18-1778..H.
131. Walter Hastings, Surgeon...............B...........3-18-1778..H.
132. Michael Jackson, Colonel...............B...........3-18-1778..H.
133. Abraham Watson, Captain..............B...........3-18-1778..H.
134. Thomas Jackson, Captain Lieutenant....B...........3-19-1778..H.
135. James Lovell, Ensign...................B...........3-19-1778..H.
136. Ebenezer Lovell, Ensign................B...........3-19-1778..H.
137. Silas Peirce, Lieutenant................B...........3-19-1778..H.
138. William Perkins, Captain...............B...........3-19-1778..H.
139. Francis Putnam, Lieutenant............B...........3-19-1778..H.
140. Benjamin Allen Upham, Surgeon's Mate..B..........3-19-1778..H.
141. John Story, Deputy Q.M.G..............B...........3-19-1778..H.
142. William Cushing, Lieutenant............B...........3-21-1778..H.
143. Joseph Fox, Captain....................B...........3-21-1778..H.
144. Robert Muzzy, Lieutenant..............B...........3-21-1778..H.
145. John Sale, Lieutenant..................B...........3-21-1778..H.
146. William Scott, Captain.................B...........3-21-1778..H.
147. Thomas Turner, Captain...............B...........3-21-1778..H.
148. Ezekiel Cheever, Commissary of Ordnance.Sf..........3-22-1778..K.
149. Joseph Eayres (Ayers), Major of Artificers.Sf..........3-22-1778..K.
150. David Mason, Director of Ordnance.....Sf..........3-22-1778..K.
151. Samuel Adams, Surgeon................B...........3-23-1778..H.
152. John Barker, Lieutenant...............B...........3-23-1778..H.
153. Thomas Bolter, Captain of Carpenters...Sf..........3-23-1778..K.
154. Edward Boylston, Captain of Wheelwrights............................Sf..........3-23-1778..K.
155. John Bryant, Captain Lieutenant........Sf..........3-23-1778..K.
156. Joshua Cheever, Conductor of Ordnance..Sf..........3-23-1778..K.
157. John Collins, Deputy Commissary of Ordnance................................Sf..........3-23-1778..K.
158. Richard Faxon, Captain of a Company of
     Smiths..............................Sf..........3-23-1778..K.
159. William Hawes, Captain of a Company of
     Harness Makers.....................Sf..........3-23-1778..K.
160. Ezra Newell (Newhall), Lieutenant......B..........3-23-1778..H.
161. Eli Parsons, First Lieutenant...........Sf..........3-23-1778..K.
162. Samuel Wild, Quarter Master of Artificers.Sf..........3-23-1778..K.
163. William Barton, Master Armourer.......Sf..........3-24-1778..K.

Library of Congress Collection 69

Page	Deponent Office		Where taken	Date	Witness
164.	Isaac Greenwood, Jr., Master Turner in Laboratory		Sf	3-24-1778	K.
165.	Samuel Henley, Lieutenant		B	3-24-1778	H.
166.	William Lowden, Master Tinman		Sf	3-24-1778	K.
167.	John Burnham, Captain		B	3-27-1778	H.
168.					
169.	William Treadwell, Captain		B	3-28-1778	H.
170.	John Clark, Jr., Major		Cln	4- 1-1778	D.
171.	Jacob Conant, Surgeon's Mate		B	4- 1-1778	H.
172.	Anthony Manne (Mann), Surgeon's Mate		B	4- 1-1778	—.
173.	Stephen Abbott, Lieutenant		B	4-11-1778	H.
174.	Armand, Marquis de la Rouerie, Colonel of an Independent Corps		B	4-11-1778	H.
175.	Louis Devrigny, Lieutenant Colonel		B	4-11-1778	H.
176.	Joseph Pettingill, Captain		B	4-11-1778	H.
177.	Joshua Lawrence, Lieutenant		B	4-13-1778	H.
178.	Richard Bagnell, Ensign		B	4-15-1778	H.
179.	Ephriam Burr, Captain		B	4-21-1778	H.
180.	Abner Howard (Hayward), Lieutenant		B	4-21-1778	H.
181.	Nicholas Gilman, Continental Loan Officer		N.H.	4-21-1778	M.W.
182.	John Cotton, Lieutenant		B	4-26-1778	H.
183.	Richard Ellis, Continental Agent for the Port of Beaufort		New Berne, N. C.	4-27-1778	D.
184.	Henry Schank, Assistant Commissary of Purchases in the Eastern Department		FK	4-27-1778	McD.
185.	James Keith, Captain		B	5- 1-1778	H.
186.	John Nixon, Brigadier General		B	5- 1-1778	H.
187.	Japhet Daniels, Captain		FK	5- 7-1778	McD.
188.	Richard Platt, Major & Aid-de-Camp		FK	5- 8-1778	McD.
188.	Ranald S. McDougall, Major & Aid-de-Camp		FK	5- 8-1778	McD.
189.	Adam Wheeler,[1] Captain		FK	5- 8-1778	McD.
189.	Nathan Wheeler,[1] Lieutenant		FK	5- 8-1778	McD.
190.	Thomas Nixon,[1] Colonel		FK	5- 8-1778	McD.
190.	Calvin Smith,[1] Lieutenant Colonel		FK	5- 8-1778	McD.
191.	William TooGood,[1] Captain		FK	5- 8-1778	McD.
191.	Samuel Fairbank,[1] Lieutenant		FK	5- 8-1778	McD.
191.	Joel Greene,[1] Lieutenant		FK	5- 8-1778	McD.
192.	Matthew Chambers,[1] Lieutenant		FK	5- 8-1778	McD.
192.	Isaac Nichols,[1] Lieutenant		FK	5- 8-1778	McD.

[1] From Massachusetts.

70   OATHS OF ALLEGIANCE

Page   Deponent   Office   Where taken   Date   Witness
192. Moses Porter,¹ Ensign...................FK........5- 8-1778..McD.
193. John Crane,¹ Lieutenant................FK........5- 8-1778..McD.
193. Stephen Fowler,¹ Ensign................FK........5- 8-1778..McD.
193. John Holden,¹ Lieutenant...............FK........5- 8-1778..McD.
194. Richard Buckmaster,¹ Adjutant.........FK........5- 8-1778..McD.
194. Samuel Jamison,¹ Quarter Master.......FK........5- 8-1778..McD.
194. Thaddeus Thompson,¹ Surgeon's Mate...FK........5- 8-1778..McD.
195. Solomon Jones,¹ Ensign.................FK........5- 8-1778..McD.
196. Joseph Bolcum,¹ Captain................FK........5- 8-1778..McD.
196. Elijah Dantford,¹ Captain..............FK........5- 8-1778..McD.
196. Benjamin Pike,¹ Lieutenant............FK........5- 8-1778..McD.
197. Dudley Tyler,¹ Lieutenant..............FK........5- 8-1778..McD.
197. Peter Clayes,¹ Lieutenant..............FK........5- 8-1778..McD.
197. Levi Holden,¹ Ensign...................FK........5- 8-1778..McD.
198. Philip Pell, Deputy Judge Advocate in
        Northern Department................FK........5- 9-1778..McD.
198. John Adams,¹ Deputy Commissary of
        Prisons in the Northern Department...FK........5- 9-1778..McD.
199. John Pierce,¹ Assistant Paymaster General
        in the Northern Department.........FK........5- 9-1778..McD.
200. Caleb Austin, Surgeon's Mate..........FK........5-11-1778..McD.
201. Cornelius Bradford, A.D.F.M.Gen.......FK........5-11-1778..McD.
202. William Dobbs, Superintendent of Black-
        smiths in the Northern Department....FK.........5-11-1778..McD.
203. Gershom Mott, Captain.................FK........5-11-1778..McD.
204. Alexander Lamb, Forage Master........FK........5-11-1778..McD.
205. Peter A. Schenk, Assistant Commissary
        of Forage............................FK........5-11-1778..McD.
206. James Townsend, Captain...............FK........5-11-1778..McD.
207. Nicholas Quackenbos, A.D.Q.M.Gen.....FK........5-11-1778..McD.
208. Thomas Weeks, Deputy Waggon Master
        General............................FK........5-11-1778..McD.
208. John Adams, Superintendent of Mechanics.FK........5-11-1778..McD.
209. Isaac Hubble, Adjutant................FK........5-11-1778..McD.
209. Francis Shaw, Lieutenant..............FK........5-11-1778..McD.
209. Shepherd Hollock, Lieutenant..........FK........5-11-1778..McD.
210. Joseph Ashton, Lieutenant.............FK........5-11-1778..McD.
210. George Leacraft, Lieutenant...........FK........5-11-1778..McD.
210. William Stachan, Lieutenant...........FK........5-11-1778..McD.
211. Lewis Dubois,² Colonel.................FK........5-11-1778..McD.
211. James Rosecrans, Captain..............FK........5-11-1778..McD.

¹ From Massachusetts.
² From New York.

Library of Congress Collection

Page	Deponent Office	Where taken	Date	Witness
211.	Daniel Birdsall	FK	5-11-1778	McD.
212.	Henry Dubois, Adjutant	FK	5-12-1778	McD.
213.	John Fitch, Assistant Commissary of Issues	FK	5-12-1778	McD.
214.	Nathan Holbrook, Lieutenant	FK	5-12-1778	McD.
215.	John Holden, Ensign	FK	5-12-1778	McD.
216.	Henry I. Vandenburgh, Ensign	FK	5-12-1778	McD.
217.	Philip D. B. Bevier, Captain	FK	5-12-1778	McD.
217.	John Lamb, Colonel	FK	5-12-1778	McD.
217.	James Stewart, Captain	FK	5-12-1778	McD.
218.	John F. Hamtranck, Captain	FK	5-12-1778	McD.
218.	James Betts, Lieutenant	FK	5-12-1778	McD.
218.	Simon English, Lieutenant	FK	5-12-1778	McD.
219.	William Boland, Assistant Commissary of Issues	FK	5-13-1778	McD.
220.	—— Hughes, Colonel & Deputy Q.M.G.	FK	5-13-1778	McD.
221.	Lewis de la Radiere, Colonel of Engineers	FK	5-13-1778	McD.
222.	Stephen Sears, Assistant Commissary of Forage	FK	5-13-1778	McD.
223.	Joseph Pierson, Assistant Commissary of Forage	FK	5-14-1778	McD.
224.	John Keese, Assistant Deputy Q.M.G.	FK	5-14-1778	McD.
224.	John Banker, Barrack Master General	FK	5-14-1778	McD.
225.	Daniel Gano, Captain Lieutenant	FK	5-14-1778	McD.
225.	Isaac Guion, Lieutenant	FK	5-14-1778	McD.
226.	Duncan Duffee, Forage Master	FK	5-16-1778	McD.
227.	George Mavings, Conductor of Ordnance and Military Stores	FK	5-16-1778	McD.
228.	Ashbill Porter, Conductor of Teams	FK	5-16-1778	McD.
229.	William Rickman, Deputy Director General	Wbg	5-16-1778	E.R.
230.	Amos Stevens, Conductor of Teams	FK	5-16-1778	McD.
231.	Thomas Barnes,[1] Captain	FK	5-18-1778	McD.
232.	Christopher Minott, Paymaster in Springfield Department	B	5-18-1778	H.
233.	Richard King, Clerk to Q.M.G.	FK	5-18-1778	McD.
234.	John Austin, Conductor of Military Stores	FK	5-21-1778	McD.
235.	John Carter,[3] Commercial Agent	Wbg	5-21-1778	E.R.
236.	Joseph Clark, Conductor of Military Stores	FK	5-21-1778	McD.

[1] From Massachusetts.
[3] From Virginia.

72   OATHS OF ALLEGIANCE

Page   Deponent   Office   Where taken   Date   Witness
237. Thomas Frothingham, Conductor of Military
       Stores.........................FK........5-21-1778..McD.
238. Thomas Gray, Conductor of Military
       Stores.........................FK........5-21-1778..McD.
239. John Ruddock, Commissary of Military
       Stores.........................FK........5-21-1778..McD.
240. Arondt Van Hook, Clerk to Ordnance
       Stores.........................FK........5-21-1778..McD.
241. John White, Assistant Commissary......FK........5-21-1778..McD.
242. Jonathan Square, Conductor of Teams...FK........5-23-1778..McD.
243. Andrew Bostwick, ———............FK........5-24-1778..McD.
244. Daniel Tein (or Teir), Assistant Commissary of Forage..................FK........5-24-1778..McD.
245. Cornelius Vellie, Assistant D.Q.M.G. of
       Forage.........................FK........5-24-1778..McD.
246. Isaac Foster, Doctor & Director General
       of Hospitals of the Eastern Department.Y.T........6- 4-1778..T.McK.
247. Thomas Edison, Clerk to the Secretary of
       Congress......................———....6-12-1778..H.L.
248. Paul Fooks, Interpreter to Congress.....———....6-23-1778..T.McK.
249. Isaac Coren, Captain.................Csl.........7-13-1778..McI.
250. Resolve Smith, Commissioner of Claims..———....10- 1-1778..T.McK.
251. Abraham Dehuff (Dekriff), Captain......L.........10- 3-1778..E.H.
252. George Bond, Clerk to the Secretary of
       Congress......................———....10-12-1778..H.L.
253. George Bond, Clerk to the Secretary of
       Congress......................———....10-12-1778..H.L.
254. (Note: The following eleven names are those of signers of an Affirmation of Allegiance. They are all on one piece of paper which is dated, "Headquarters, Little Egg Harbour, 10-21-1778." In the "Alphabetical Index of Signers of the Oath of Allegiance," refered to elsewhere herein, as being in the Library of Congress, these men are all designated "Quakers.")

            Silas Ireland   Samuel Parker
            Cajah Willetts   Joseph King
            Noah Ridgwa   Peter Parker
            Stephen Ayers   James Cramer
            Joseph Parker   Edward Parker
                          Adam Pettitt

255. William Geddes, Commissioner of Accounts.........................Ph........11-23-1778..T.McK.
256. William Geddes, Commissioner of Accounts.........................Ph........11-24-1778..H.L.

Library of Congress Collection 73

Page	Deponent Office	Where taken	Date	Witness
257.	Joshua Coit, Clerk to the Secretary of Congress................................	——	4- 3-1778	J.J.
258.	Charles Morse, Clerk to the Secretary of Congress................................	——	6- 9-1778	J.J.
259.	John Jackson, Clerk to the Secretary of Congress................................	——	9- 3-1778	J.J.
260.	Aaron D. Woodruff, Clerk to the Secretary of Congress......................	Ph	10-20-1778	S.H.
261.	John Gibson, Commissioner of the Treasury.............................	Ph	11-27-1778	S.H.
262.	Ezekiel Foreman, Commissioner of the Treasury.............................	Ph	12-18-1778	S.H.
263.	James Milligan, Auditor General of the Treasury.............................	——	12-27-1778	S.H.
264.	Charles Lee, Secretary of the Board of the Treasury of the United States.......	Ph	4- 4-1780	S.H.
265.	William Denning, Commissioner of the Treasury of the United States.......	——	6- 3-1780	S.H.
266.	William Paca, Judge in the Court of Capture...................................	Ph	6-15-1780	S.H.
266.	Cyrus Griffin, Judge in the Court of Capture...................................	Ph	6-15-1780	S.H.
267.	Peter R. Fell, Commissioner of Accounts	Ph	6-21-1780	S.H.
268.	George Measam, Commissioner of Accounts...........................	Ph	6-21-1780	S.H.
269.	Jonathan Burrall, Commissioner of Accounts...........................	Ph	6-22-1780	S.H.
270.	James McCall, Commissioner of Accounts	Ph	8- 3-1780	S.H.
271.	Timothy Pickering, Quarter Master General..............................	Ph	8- 9-1780	T.McK.
272.	Timothy Pickering, Quarter Master General..............................	Ph	8- 9-1780	T.McK.
273.	Michael Hillegas, Treasurer of the United States.................................	——	8-10-1780	S.H.
274.	Charles Pettit, Assistant Q.M.G.........	Ph	8-22-1780	T.McK.
275.	Charles Pettit, Assistant Q.M.G.........	Ph	8-22-1780	T.McK.
276.	Ebenezer Smith, Clerk to the Secretary of Congress.............................	——	12-30-1780	S.H.
277.	Patrick Ferrall, Clerk to the Auditor General..............................	——	1-19-1781	G.B.
278.	John Sanford Dart, Auditor of the Army	Ph	1-31-1781	S.H.
279.	John Sanford Dart, Auditor of the Army	Ph	1-31-1781	S.H.
280.	Matthew McConnel, Captain...........	Ph	2-21-1781	W.I.

74   Oaths of Allegiance

Page	Deponent Office	Where taken	Date	Witness
281.	John Pierce, Paymaster General	Ph	4-16-1781	B.P.
282.	Henry Remsen, Jr., Clerk to the Secretary of Congress	—	5-20-1781	S.H.
283.	Robert Morris, Superintendent of Finances of the United States	—	6-27-1781	McK.
284.	Robert Morris, Superintendent of Finances of the United States	Ph	6-27-1781	McK.
285.	Thomas Hutchins, Geographer of the United States	Ph	5-25-1781	McK.
286.	Gouverneur Morris, Assistant to the Suintendent of Finances of the United States	—	8- 7-1781	McK.
287.	Gouverneur Morris, Assistant to the Superintendent of Finances of the United States	—	8- 7-1781	McK.
288.	Benjamin Bankson, Clerk to the Secretary of Congress	—	8-18-1781	McK.
289.	Joseph Nourse, Register of Accounts	—	10-12-1781	McK.
290.	Robert R. Livingston, Secretary of Foreign Affairs	Ph	10-20-1781	McK.
291.	Peter Stephen Du Ponceau, Secretary to the Secretary of Foreign Affairs	Ph	10-22-1781	McK.
292.	William Ramsay, Clerk in the Comptroller's Office	Ph	10-25-1781	McK.
293.	Patrick Ferrall, Clerk in the Office of the Comptroller	Ph	10-25-1781	McK.
294.	James Milligan, Comptroller	Ph	10-25-1781	McK.
295.	Cornelius Conegys, Clerk in the Comptroller's Office	Ph	10-30-1781	McK.
296.	Lewis R. Morris, Secretary in the Office of the Secretary of Foreign Affairs	Ph	11-16-1781	McK.
297.	William Simmons, Clerk in the Comptroller's Office	—	11-21-1781	J.S.H.
298.	Benjamin Lincoln, Secretary of War	—	11-30-1781	J.S.H.
299.	George Hopes, Clerk in the Comptroller's Office	—	12-11-1781	J.S.H.
300.	John L. Clarkson, Secretary to Superintendent of Finance	—	1-11-1782	J.S.H.
301.	William Geddes, Auditor in the Treasury Department	—	2- 2-1782	J.S.H.
302.	John D. Mercier, Auditor in the Treasury Department	—	2- 2-1782	J.S.H.
303.	Guilliam Aertsen, Clerk of Accounts	—	2- 6-1782	J.S.H.

Library of Congress Collection

Page	Deponent Office	Where taken	Date	Witness
304.	James McCall, Secretary to Superintendent of Finance	——	2- 1-1782	J.S.H.
305.	James Dundas, Clerk of Accounts	——	2-25-1782	G.B.
306.	Daniel Brodhead, Clerk to the Superintendent of Finance	——	3-18-1782	J.S.H.
307.	John Peter Tetard, Clerk to the Secretary of Foreign Affairs	Ph	4-16-1782	McK.
308.	Jonathan Burrall, Commissioner	——	5-18-1782	B.P.
309.	Spencer Roane, Clerk to the Superintendent of Finance	——	6-20-1782	McK.
310.	Edward Wright, Jr., Clerk to the Superintendent of Finance	——	9- 9-1782	McK.
311.	George Turner, Commissary of Marine Prisons	——	10-19-1782	P.F.
312.	Edward Fox, Commissioner for settling Hospital Accounts	——	10-24-1782	J.S.H.
313.	Joseph Bindon, Commissioner for settling the Clothiers' Accounts	——	10-26-1782	J.S.H.
314.	Ebenezer Hazard, Post Master General of the United States	Ph	11- 1-1782	J.S.H.
315.	Robert Smock, Clerk in the Office for settling Clothiers' Accounts	Ph	11- 8-1782	J.S.H.
316.	John Lawrence, Clerk in the Office for settling Commissary Accounts	——	11-11-1782	B.P.
317.	Walter Stone, Clerk to the Secretary of Foreign Affairs	——	2-25-1783	McK.
318.	George Read, Judge in the Court of Appeals in Cases of Capture	——	4-14-1783	E.B.
319.	Thomas Wiggans, Clerk to the Commissioner to settle Clothiers' Accounts	Ph	4-28-1783	W.A.
320.	John Lowell, Judge of the Court of Appeals in Cases of Capture	——	5-27-1783	E.B.
321.	Henry Remsen, Jr., Under Secretary of Foreign Affairs	Maryland	3- 5-1784	A.H.
322.	John Kilty, Jr., Clerk in the Secretary's Office	Maryland	3-12-1784	A.C.
323.	John Jay, Secretary of Foreign Affairs	Trenton, N. J.	12-25-1784	I.S.
324.	Charles D. Remsen, Clerk in the Office of the Secretary of Congress	N.Y.	1-20-1785	Brm.
325.	Abraham Okie (Oakey), "of the City of New York," Taylor, Doorkeeper and Messenger in the Office of the Secretary of Foreign Affairs	——	2- 1-1785	W.N.

76   OATHS OF ALLEGIANCE

Page   Deponent   Office   Where taken   Date   Witness
326. Jacob Blackwell, Clerk in the Office of the
     Secretary of Foreign Affairs...........N.Y........2- 8-1785..J.B.
327. John Fisher, Clerk to the Secretary of
     Congress...........................———.....2- 8-1785..C.T.
328. John Swaine, Printer of the United States.———.....2-22-1785..C.T.
329. Benjamin Walker, Lieutenant Colonel &
     Interpreter of Foreign Languages......———.....2-24-1785..C.T.
330. George Taylor, Jr., Clerk in the Office of
     Foreign Affairs......................N.Y........3- 1-1785..R.V.
331. Walter Livingston, Commissioner of the
     Board of Treasury...................N.Y........—————..J.D.
332. Samuel Osgood, Commissioner of the
     Board of Treasury...................N.Y........4- 9-1785..J.D.
333. Henry Knox, Secretary of War..........N.Y........4-25-1785..J.S.H.
334. John Pintard, Interpreter..............———.....5- 5-1785..J.B.
335. John Christopher Kunze, Interpreter.....———.....5-10-1785..C.T.
336. Joseph Carlton, Secretary in War Office..———.....5-18-1785..C.T.
337. Robert Pemberton, Clerk in the War
     Office..............................———.....5-20-1785..C.T.
338. Arthur Lee, Commissioner of the Board
     of Treasury.........................———.....9- 8-1785..J.H.
339. Samuel Shaw, Secretary in the War Office.———....11- 7-1785..C.T.
340. John Stagg, Jr., Clerk in the War Office..———.....3-23-1786..C.T.
341. Richard Butler, Superintendent of Indian
     Affairs.............................N.Y.......10-10-1786..J.S.H.
342. James White, Superintendent of Indian
     Affairs.............................———....10-10-1786..J.S.H.
343. Johann Daniel Gros, Interpreter.........———....11- 6-1786..C.T.
344. Isaac Pinto, Interpreter (Spanish).......———....11-30-1786..C.T.
345. Arthur Lee, Commissioner of Board of
     Treasury............................———.....——-1787..R.M.
346. Samuel Osgood, Commissioner of Board of
     Treasury............................———....11-10-1787..R.M.
347. Samuel Osgood, Commissioner of
     Treasury............................———....11-10-1787..R.M.
348. Arthur St. Clair, Governor of the Terri-
     tory of the United States West of the
     River Ohio..........................N.Y........2- 7-1788..C.G.
249. John Cleve Symmes, One of the Judges of
     the Territory of the United States West
     of the River Ohio....................———.....3-26-1788..St.C.
350. Richard Winn, Superintendent of Indian
     Affairs for the Southern District.......South
                                          Carolina..3-31-1788..J.Bru.

Page	Deponent Office	Where taken	Date	Witness
351.	Samuel Holden Parsons, One of the Judges of the Territory of the United States West of the River Ohio...............	———	..... 4- 4-1788	..St.C.
352.	James Mitchell Varnum, One of the Judges of the Territory of the United States West of the River Ohio...............	———	..... 4- 4-1788	..St.C.
353.	Winthrop Sargent, Secretary "in and for" the Territory of the United States West of the River Ohio....................	———	....10- 8-1788	..St.C.
354.	"We, William Irvine, John Taylor Gilman, and Abraham Baldwin, appointed a board of Commissioners for settling the accounts between the United States and Individual States"....................	———	1-19-1809	..R.M.

York Town February 21ˢᵗ 1778

This may certify that before me the Honorable Thomas McKean Esqʳ Chief Justice of the State of Pennsylvania, William Govett of St Judes to genereal has this day taken and subscribed the Affirmation of Allegiance to the United States of America, directed by the Resolutions of Congress of the third instant

Tho. M. Kean

Affirmation of William Govett.

INDEX

This index is prepared with reference to the sources from which the material in this volume is compiled. These sources are: First, a collection in the War Department Records in the National Archives composed of four albums wherein the individual oaths are numbered. Second, a collection in the Library of Congress each oath of which collection is numbered. In this index the number which precedes a name is the number of the volume containing that oath in the National Archives collection and the number which follows the name is that of the individual oath. Where an oath is to be found in the Library of Congress collection, the symbol *lc* preceeds the name and the number of the individual oath follows the name. Ex. *lc*. Abbot, Stephen 173, means that the oath of Stephen Abbot is in the Library of Congress and is numbered 173. Or 166, Adams, David 389 means that the oath of David Adams is in Vol. 166 in the War Department Records in the National Archives and is numbered 389 in that volume.

A

- *lc.* Abbot, Stephen, 173
- 166. Adams, David, 389
- 167. Adams, Francis, 260
- *lc.* Adams, John, 198, 208.
- *lc.* Adams, Samuel, 151
- *lc.* Aertsen, Guilliam, 303
- 166. Alden, Ichabod, 329
- 167. Alden, Roger, 98
- 168. Allen, David, 606
- 165. Allen, James, 167, 226
- 166. Allen, Nathaniel Coit, 461
- 166. Allen, William, 437
- 168. Allison, John, 423
- 168. Allison, Richard, 503
- 167. Amberson, William, 298
- 167. Andrews, James, 103
- 168. Anderson, John, 377
- 167. Anderson, Jos. T., 4
- 168. Anderson, Nathaniel, 381
- 168. Anderson, Richard C., 611
- 167. Anderson, Richard, 144
- 166. Anderson, Thomas, 594.
- *lc.* Archibald, Edward, 56.
- *lc.* Armand, Marquis de la Rouerie, 174
- 165. Arnold, Benedict, 5
- 166. Arnold, Samuel, 397
- 166. Arnold, Thomas, 423
- 168. Alexander, Archibald, 397
- 167. Alexander, John, 304
- 165. Alexander, Thomas, 149, 235
- 168. Apperson, Richard, 457
- 168. Armistead, Thomas, 413
- 166. Armstrong, Edward, 360
- 168. Armstrong, James, 492
- 166. Armstrong, John, 597
- 167. Armstrong, Thomas, 149
- 165. Armstrong, William, 193, 119
- 167. Armstrong, William, 171
- 166. Ashby, Benjamin, 382
- 168. Ashmead, Jacob, 477
- 167. Ashton, John, 288
- *lc.* Ashton, Joseph, 210
- *lc.* Austin Caleb, 200
- *lc.* Austin, John, 234
- 167. Avery, Simeon, 86

B

- *lc.* Bache, Richard, 99, 100
- 167. Bacot, Peter, 166
- *lc.* Bagnell, Richard, 178
- 165. Baker, George A., 139, 240
- *lc.* Baldwin, Abraham, 354
- 167. Baldwin, Caleb, 45
- *lc.* Baldwin, Jeduthan, 87
- 167. Ball, Blackall William, 234
- 168. Ball, Burges, 593.
- 165. Ballard, Benjamin, 153, 246
- 167. Ballard, Jeremiah, 16
- 167. Ballard, Kedar, 135
- 168. Ballard, Robert, 596
- 166. Ballard, William Hudson, 324
- 168. Balmain, Alexander, 380
- 166. Baltzel, Charles, 551
- 167. Banks, Joseph, 251
- *lc.* Bankson, Benjamin, 288
- 168. Bankson, John, 469
- *lc.* Banker, John, 224
- *lc.* Bannister, Seth, 101
- 168. Barbee, Thomas, 407
- 167. Barber, Francis, 3
- *lc.* Barber, Nathaniel, Junr., 41
- 165. Barber, William, 53, 87
- 165. Barclay, James, 262
- *lc.* Barker, John, 152
- *lc.* Barker, Thomas, 77

166. Barnes, Daniel, 405
167. Barnes, James, 44
lc. Barnes, Thomas, 231
168. Barnett, James, 465
167. Barnum, Samuel, 43
166. Barret, Chiswell, 386
168. Bartholomew, Benjamin, 516
168. Bartley, John, 509
lc. Barton, William, 163
168. Baskerville, Thomas, 404
166. Basset, Barachiah, 526
166. Bates, Joseph, 519
166. Batman, William, 485
165. Baugh, Robert, 151, 248
168. Baxter, William, 360
167. Bayard, Stephen, 295
166. Bayer, Michael, 545
165. Bayles, Hodijah, 41
168. Baytop, John, 450
166, Beach (Beech), William, 529
168. Beale (Beall), Robert, 367, 388
167. Beardsley, Phineas, 36
168. Beatty, E., 499
167. Bebee, James, 102
165. Belole (Belote) Noah, 263
166. Belote (Belole), Noah, 289
lc. Benezet, John, 2
166. Benjamin, Aaron, 393
167. Bensted, Alexander, 259
168. Bentley, William, 378
166. Benton, Selah, 418
168. Best, John, 418
lc. Betts, James, 218
167. Betts, Stephen, 116
lc. Bevier, Philip D. B., 217
168. Bicker, Henry, 478
167. Bickman, James, 207
165. Biddle, Clement, 97, 100
168. Biggs, Benjamin, 586
lc. Biggs, Thomas, 79
166. Bill, Beriah, 428
167. Billing, Stephen, 34
lc. Bindon, Joseph, 313
165. Binney, Barnabas, 180
lc. Bird, Mark, 8.
lc. Birdsall, Daniel, 211
167. Birkman, John, 284
166. Bishop, Nathaniel, 415
168. Black, James, 401
166. Black, James, 349
lc. Blackwell, Jacob, 326
168. Blackwell, Joseph, 399
167. Blackwell, Robert, 318
168. Blackwell, Thomas, 403
167. Blair, John, 301

166. Bland, Theo. M., 348
167. Bloomfield, Joseph, 10
lc. Bodlam, Ezra, 112
lc. Boland, William, 219
lc. Bolcum, Joseph, 196
lc. Bolter, Thomas, 153
lc. Bond, George, 252, 253
167. Bonham, Absolem, 33
168. Boswell, Machen, 410
lc. Bostwick, Andrew, 243
168. Boude, Thomas, 505
167. Bowen, Thomas Bartholomew, 272
168. Bower, Jacob, 356
167. Bowman, Joshua, 162
168. Bowne, Thomas, 537
167. Boyd, Adam, 176, 235
166. Boyd, Thomas, 381
167. Boyer, Benjamin, 105
168. Boyer, Peter, 605
lc. Boylston, Edward, 154
lc. Bradford, Cornelius, 201
166. Bradford, Gamaliel, 525
lc. Bradford, Robert, 113
165. Bradford, William, 85
168. Brady, Samuel, 326
168. Brahan, John, 621
167. Bradley, Daniel, 63
166. Bramhall, Joshua, 467
167. Brearly, David, 22
168. Brent, William, 422
168. Bressie, Thomas, 580
166. Brewer, Samuel, 473
166. Brigham, Paul, 433
167. Brodhead, Daniel, 296
lc. Brodhead, Daniel, 306
168. Brodhead, Luke, 343
168. Brodie (Broady), Lodowick, 581
166. Brodrick, James, 531
lc. Brown, Andrew, 42
166. Brown, Daniel, 449
168. Brown, David, 498
166. Brown, Ezekiel, 292
165. Brown, Gawen, 71
167. Brown, John, 168
167. Brown, Joseph, 222
167. Brown, Samuel, 87
166. Brown, Sylvanus, 426
168. Brown, Windsor, 420
167. Brownlee, Joseph, 213
lc. Bryant, John, 155
166. Buck, John, 494
lc. Buckmaster, Richard, 194
165. Budd, Isaac, 89
167. Budd, Samuel, 180
166. Buffington, Samuel, 330

INDEX

168. Buford, Abraham, 554
166. Bull, William, 533
166. Bullard, Asa, 465
168. Bunner, Rudolph, 480
166. Bunner, Jacob, 548
168. Burd, Benjamin, 502
168. Burfoot, Thomas, 574
166. Burkhard, Daniel, 550
lc. Burkman, Thomas, 120
166. Burley, William, 518
lc. Burnham, John, 167
166. Burnham, Samuel, 341
166. Burr, Aaron, 591
lc. Burr, Ephriam, 179
lc. Burrell, Jonathan, 308
165. Burroughs, George, 185, 243
167. Bush, John, 305
166. Buss, Samuel, 450
lc. Bussey, Isaiah, 121
lc. Butler, Anthony, 16
168. Butler, Percival, 482
167. Butler, Richard, 282
lc. Butler, Richard, 341
168. Butler, Thomas, 488
168. Butler, William, 496
166. Buxton, James, 456
165. Buyers, George, 201, 271

C

168. Cabell, Samuel I., 558
167. Calhoun, George, 257½
165. Calhoun, James, 132, 140
165. Calhoun, John, 145
166. Call, Richard, 576
lc. Callender, John, 46
167. Callender, Thomas, 118
168. Calmes, Marcus, 441
165. Campbell, George W., 122
167. Campbell, James, 172
165. Campbell, John, 169, 224
168. Campbell, Richard, 393
168. Campbell, Samuel, 571
168. Campbell, William, 427
165. Carew, James, 52
lc. Carlton, Joseph, 336
166. Carlton, Samuel, 470
167. Carnahan, James, 204
lc. Carnes, Thomas J., 88
166. Carter, (McCarter), Charles, 375
lc. Carter, John, 235.
166. Carter, Stephen, 331
165. Cartwright, Thomas, 74
165. Castaign (see Lagrace), Peter, 58
168. Catlett, Thomas, 437
167. Catlin, Eli, 69

lc. Chace, Thomas, 47
165. Chaloner, John, 233
167. Chamberlin, Ephriam, 38
168. Chambers, James, 330
lc. Chambers, Matthew, 192
167. Chambers, Stephen, 232
167. Chapman, Elijah, 72
166. Charles, Joseph, 294
165. Chase, Dudley L., 134
165. Cheesborough, John, 158, 219
lc. Cheever, Ezekiel, 148
lc. Cheever, Joshua, 156
166. Cheney, William, 319
167. Child, Josiah, 74
166. Childs, Isaac, 508
167. Chipman, Nathaniel, 101
168. Christy, John, 510
168. Chrystie, James, 489
lc. Church, Alexander, 48
168. Church, Thomas, 495
168. Claiborne, Richard, 548
165. Clark, Ebenezer, 247
167. Clark, John, 202
lc. Clark, John, Junr., 170
lc. Clark, Joseph, 236
166. Clark, Silas, 445
167. Clark, Thomas, 157
168. Clark, Thomas, 588
lc. Clarkson, John L., 300
165. Clarkson, Matthew, 29
168. Clay, Matthew, 364
lc. Clayes, Peter, 197
lc. Claypool, D. C., 1
168. Claypool, William, 352
166. Cleft, Lemuel, 402
167. Cleveland, Moses, 100
166. Cleveland, Timothy, 403
168. Clifton, Robert, 323
168. Cobbs, Samuel, 444
166. Coburn, Asa, 301
165. Cochran, John, 83
lc. Cogswell, Samuel, 127
lc. Coit, Joshua, 257
168. Cole, George, 609
168. Cole, John, 433
167. Cole, John, 268
165. Cole, Thomas, 260
166. Cole, Thomas, 284
167. Coleman, Benjamin, 156
167. Coleman, Charles, 159
166. Coleman, Edmund, 419
167. Coleman, Nicholas, 278
168. Coleman, Wyatt, 416
165. Colfax, William, 34
167. Collier, Joseph, 217

168. Collins, Bartlet, 578
lc. Collins, John, 157
lc. Colman, Dudley, 78
166. Colman, John, 379
168. Colston, Samuel, 376
166. Colton, Charles, 297
166. Comstock, Samuel, 424
lc. Conant, Jacob, 171
166. Conant, Jonathan, 512
lc. Condy, Thomas Hollis, 57
lc. Conegys, Cornelius, 295
167. Conger, Joseph, 182
167. Conn, Samuel, 18
lc. Connelly, Michael, 58
165. Connor, Charles, 113, 209¾
167. Converse, Thomas, 35
167. Conway, John, 29
168. Conway, Joseph, 552
167. Coots, James, 160
lc. Coren, Isaac, 249
165. Corvell, John, 107
167. Cotgrove, Arthur, 137
lc. Cotton, John, 182
167. Council, Robert, 143
lc. Courtis, William, 92
168. Cowherd, Francis, 435
165. Cox, John, 98, 137
167. Cox, Richard, 9
167. Cox, William, 249
167. Craddock, John, 134
166. Craig, John, 567
168. Craig, Samuel, 333
168. Craig, Thomas, 479
165. Craik, James, 36, 37
166. Cramer, Jacob, 549
lc. Crane, John, 193
167. Craven, James, 127
168. Crawford, Edward, 321
168. Crawford, John, 436
167. Crawford, John, 294
166. Crawford, Thomas, 291
165. Crawford, Thomas, 272
lc. Creamer, James, 254
lc. Crequi, Peter M., 89
lc. Crocker, Joseph, 129
166. Cronen, Patrick, 354
165. Crosby, Ebenezer, 127
lc. Crosher, John, 90
165. Crow, Henry, 116
168. Cruize, Walter, 347
168. Crump, Abner, 414
166. Culbertson, James, 372
lc. Cumberson, Philetus, 33
166. Cummings, Thomas, 462
166. Cumpston, Edward, 345

168. Cunningham, William, 528
168. Currell, Nicholas, 363
168. Curtis, Thomas, 359
166. Curtis, William, 306
lc. Cushing, Nathaniel, 122
lc. Cushing, William, 142
165. Cutting, John Brown, 46, 95

D

166. Dandridge, Alexander S., 575
lc. Daniels, Japhet, 187
lc. Dantford, Elijah, 196
165. Darah, James, 176, 216
168. Darragh, Charles, 615
167. Darragh, Daniel, 283
lc. Dart, John Sanford, 278, 279
166. Davey, John, 532
168. Davidson, James, 519
168. Davie, Peter, 573
168. Davies, William, 567
166. Davis, James, 340
167. Davis, John, 290
lc. Davis, Joshua, 59
lc. Davis, Robert, 114
167. Davis, Samuel, 275
165. Davis, William, 62
lc. Dawes, William, 80
167. Dawson, Samuel, 237
167. Day, Aaron, 15
166. Day, Elijah, 310
167. Day, Isaac, 113
166. Day, Luke, 322
166. Day, Samuel, 342
lc. Dean, Thomas, 123
lc. Dearborn, Henry, 43
168. De Benneville, Daniel, 392
lc. Dehuff (or Dekriff), Abraham, 251
lc. Denning, William, 265
167. Dennis, Daniel, 252
165. Des Espiner, Augustus Francis, 48
lc. Devrigny, Louis, 175
168. Dickey, Alexander, 540
168. Dickinson, Edmund B., 523
167. Dickinson, Richard, 195
168. Dillard, James, 398
lc. Dobbs, William, 202
166. Dodge, Levi, 451
166. Dodge, Reuben, 452
166. Donnell, James, 477
lc. Donnell, Zaccheus, 49
165. Dolliver, Peter, 72
166. Dorrance, David, 596
166. Dorsey, Larkin, 566
167. Douglass, Richard, 81
166. Dow, Alexander, 356

INDEX

168. Doyl, John, 332
168. Doyl, Thomas, 336
166. Drake, Joshua, 352
165. Draper, George, 84
168. Drewry (Drury), John, 534
167. Drummond, Peter, 253
lc. Dubois, Henry, 212
lc. Dubois, Lewis, 211
168. Dudley, H., 579
168. Dudley, John, 576
168. Duff, Edward, 374
lc. Duffee, Duncan, 226
lc. Dunckerly, Joseph, 60
lc. Dundas, James, 305
167. Dungan, Thomas, 229
lc. Dunham, George, 102
lc. Dunlap, John, 1
lc. Du Ponceau, Peter Stephen, 291
165. Du Ponceau, Peter Stephen, 44
165. Du Portail, Louis, (the Chevalier) 22
165. Durie, Thomas, 163, 209½
166. Durkee, John, 399
166. Durkee, Robert, 411
166. Dyer, (Dyre), Joseph, 285
165. Dyer, Joseph, 269

E

lc. Eayers, Joseph, 149
166. Eddy, Joshua, 515
166. Edison, Thomas, 552
lc. Edison, Thomas, 247
166. Edsall, Richard, 538
165. Edwards, Thomas, 50
165. Ehrenzeller, Jacob, 49
165. Eldridge, Stephen, 282, 198
167. Ellis, John, 47
lc. Ellis, Richard, 183
166. Emerson, Nehemiah, 509
167. Engel, Andrew, 230
166. Englis, Andrew, 493
lc. English, Simeon, 218
Epiniers, see Des Epinier
168. Eppes, William, 561
lc. Eustis, Benjamin, 96
166. Evans, Elijah, 380
168. Evans, William, 452
165. Evans, William, 194, 268
168. Ewell, Thomas, 425
168. Ewing, Alexander, 575
lc. Ewing, Jasper, 103

F

lc. Fairbank, Samuel, 191
167. Faircloth, William, 184

168. Falkner, Rudolph, 445
165. Fallon, James, 182, 214
166. Fanning, Charles, 395
165. Farley, Michael, 154, 245
167. Farmer, Lewis, 197
166. Farnum, David, 464
165. Farrin (Farran), Francis, 279
165. Farron, (see Farrin)
168. Fauntleroy, Henry, 591
lc. Faxon, Richard, 158
168. Febiger, Christian, 446
lc. Fell, Peter R., 267
167. Feltman, William, 254
167. Fenner, Robert, 177
167. Fenner, William, 150
lc. Fenno, William, 104
167. Fenton, Solomon, 109
167. Ferebee, Joseph, 181
166. Fernald, Tobias, 471
lc. Ferrall, Patrick, 277, 293
167. Finley, Joseph, 199
166. Finley, Samuel, 528
167. Finny, Thomas, 179
166. Fish, Adam, 523
168. Fishbourn, Ben:, 494
lc. Fisher, John, 327
167. Fiss, Jacob, 246
166. Fitch, Andrew, 422
lc. Fitch, John, 213
168. Fitzgerald, John, 366
lc. Fitzsimmons, Jacob, 18
lc. Fitzsimmons, Thomas, 2
166. Flagg, Ebenezer, 430
Fleet, see Flut
168. Flut, John, 412
165. Flynn, John, 171, 223
lc. Fooks, Paul, 248
166. Foot, Joseph, 511
lc. Foreman, Ezekiel, 262
167. Forman, Jonathan, 27
165. Forsyth, Robert, 99, 103
lc. Fosdick, Thomas, 72
lc. Foster, Isaac, 246
168. Foster, John, 353
168. Fowler, Stephen, 193
168. Fowler, William, 373
lc. Fox, Edward, 312
lc. Fox, Joseph, 143
168. Fox, Thomas, 405
166. Francis, Aaron, 513
166. Francis, John, 505
165. Franks, David S., 30
168. Frazer, Persifer, 341
166. Frost, William, 480
lc. Frothingham, Benjamin, 105

lc. Frothingham, Richard, 106
lc. Frothingham, Thomas, 237

G

166. Gage, Isaac, 299
165. Gamble, James, 159, 249
lc. Gano, Daniel, 225
166. Gardiner, Joseph, 474
168. Gaskins, Thomas, 370
lc. Gates, Horatio, 17
167. Gatlin, Levi, 193
lc. Geddes, William, 255, 256, 301
165. Gibbs, Caleb, 32
lc. Gibson, John, 9, 261
168. Gibson, John, 461
167. Gifford, William, 2
165. Gilchrist, Adam, 131, 253
166. Gildersleeve, Finch, 367
168. Gillison, John, 406
lc. Gilman, John Taylor, 354
lc. Gilman, Nicholas, 181
167. Girard, Charles, 130
166. Givens, Robert, 308
168. Glentworth, James, 345
167. Goodman, William, 175
166. Goodridge, Samuel, 517
168. Gordon, Arthur, 384
165. Gordon, Henry, 206, 264
167. Gorman, Joseph, 216
167. Gosner, Peter, 107
lc. Govett, William, 10
165. Grace, Jacob, 203, 261
166. Granger, Bildad, 410
167. Grant, George, 286
166. Gray, George, 574
167. Gray, Nigal, 227
167. Gray, Robert, 201
lc. Gray, Thomas, 238
165. Gray, William, 202, 275
lc. Greaton, John, 35
168. Green, Benjamin, 525
168. Green, Burwell, 550
168. Green, John, 395
167. Green, William, 73
lc. Greene, Joel, 191
165. Greene, Nathaneal, 3, 4
166. Greenleaf, Moses, 503
lc. Greenwood, Isaac, Jr., 164
167. Gregg, John, 212
168. Gregg, Robert, 512
167. Gregory, Demcey, 188
lc. Gridley, Richard, 36
167. Grier, James, 261
lc. Griffin, Cyrus, 266
lc. Gros, Johan Daniel, 343

167. Grover, Phineas, 51
165. Grymes, Benjamin, 35
lc. Guion, Isaac, 225
167. Gyger (Guyger), George, 206

H

165. Hacket, Patrick, 142, 239
167. Hait, Samuel, 68
167. Hall, Clement, 139
167. Hall, Philemon, 41
167. Hall, Stephen, 50
166. Hallam, Robert, 425
166. Hallett, Jonah, 589
165. Hamilton, Alexander, 25
165. Hamilton, James, 106
168. Hamilton, James, 402
168. Hamilton, Thomas, 426
166. Hammitt, John, 537
168. Hamond, David, 324
lc. Hamtrank, John F., 218
lc. Hancock, Ebenezer, 50
166. Hanly, Henry, 376
167. Hanson, Samuel, 178
168. Hard, Thomas, 396
166. Hardin, (Harding), John, 373
167. Hargis, Abraham, 257
167. Hargrave, William, 194
168. Harkley, John, 453
168. Harmar, Josiah, 342
166. Harmon, John, 421
167. Harney, Selby, 152
167. Harris, Jacob, 32
168. Harrison, John, 603
167. Harrison, John, 154
165. Harrison, Robert H., 23
165. Hartman, Peter, 191, 212
167. Harvy, Ithamer, 96
165. Harvey, Michael, 108, 109
166. Haskell, Elnathan, 459
lc. Haskell, Henry, 81
166. Haskell, Jonathan, 468
lc. Hastings, John, 62
lc. Hastings, Walter, 131
166. Hasty, William, 504
166. Hawes, Samuel, 344
lc. Hawes, William, 159
165. Hawks, William, 77
167. Hay, Samuel, 316
lc. Haynes, Aaron, 61
lc. Hays, Moses, 26
166. Hayser (Heiser), William, 547
Hayward, see Howard
lc. Hazard, Ebenezer, 314
166. Heard, John, Junr., 577
lc. Heath, William, 37

INDEX   85

167. Heimberg, Frederick, 124
167. Henderson, Matt:, 292
168. Henderson, William, 500
165. Henderson, William, 82
166. Henry, John, 554
167. Henshaw, William, 67
167. Herbert, Stewart, 231
167. Hicks, Jacob Giles, 245
167. Higgins, Cornelius, 65
lc. Henley, Samuel, 165
167. Hill, Henry, 84
lc. Hillegass, Michael, 273
167. Hills, Ebenezer, 53
167. Hilton, William, 122
166. Hinderson, John, 565
165. Hinderson, Joseph, 111
166. Hinderson, Joseph, 286
lc. Hindes, Bartlet, 82
166. Hitchcock, Luke, 483
lc. Hitzelheimer, William, 51
165. Hobby, John, 64
166. Hodge, Asahel, 409
168. Hogg, Samuel, 604
166. Hoit (Hoyt), Joseph, 439
lc. Holbrook, Nathan, 214
166. Holden, Aaron, 332
lc. Holden, John, 193, 215
lc. Holden, Levi, 197
168. Holland, George, 570
167. Hollenbeak, John, 48
167. Holmes, Eliphalet, 97
168. Holt, Thomas, 527, 569
166. Holt, Silas, 401
166. Hoogland, Jeronemus, 559
168. Hoomes, Benjamin, 439
168. Hoomes, Thomas C., 417
167. Hooper, Robert, 258
lc. Hopkins, David, 63
168. Hopkins, Samuel, 466
lc. Hopkinson, Francis, 12
lc. Hollock, Shepherd, 209
lc. Hopes, George, 299
167. Horn, Benjamin, 14
lc. Howard, Abner, 180
lc. Hubble, Isaac, 209
166. Hubbell (Hubble), John, 490
167. Hubley, Adam, 265
168. Hudson, William, 460
168. Hughes, Greenberry, 354
167. Hughes, John, 317, 319
166. Hughes, John, 571
166. Hughes, Thomas, 427
lc. Hughes, —, 220
168. Huling, John, 490
lc. Hunnewell, Richard, 52

lc. Hunt, Abraham, 115
lc. Hunt, William, 107
167. Hunter, Andrew, 30
166. Hunter, Robert, 351
167. Huntington, Jedidiah, 99
lc. Hutchins, Thomas, 285
165. Hutchinson, James, 129

I

167. Ingles, John, 141
165. Ingram, John, 195, 270
lc. Ireland, Silas, 254
lc. Irvine, Mat:, 64
167. Irvine, Andrew, 308
167. Irvine, William, 303
lc. Irvine, William, 354
168. Irwin, John, 619

J

lc. Jackson, Henry, 44
lc. Jackson, John, 259
165. Jackson, John, 66
lc. Jackson, Michael, 132
166. Jackson, Nathan P., 408
lc. Jackson, Thomas, 134
166. Jameson, John, 582
lc. Jamison, Samuel, 194
165. Janes, Elijah, 138, 238
165. Jarvis, Nathaniel, 73
lc. Jay, John, 323
168. Jenkins, George, 338
168. Jenkins, William, 562
166. Jenks, Oliver, 414
166. Johnson, David, 396
167. Johnson, Jonathan, 59
168. Johnson, John B., 560
167. Johnson, Seth, 23
167. Johnson, William, 215
168. Johnston, Andrew, 320
168. Johnston, Francis, 513
168. Johnston, James, 473
166. Jones, Churchill, 581
168. Jones, David, 497
168. Jones, James, 493
168. Jones, James Morris, 613
166. Jones, John, 506
168. Jones, Peter, 565
167. Jones, Samuel, 136
lc. Jones, Solomon, 195
165. Jones, Thomas, 172, 220
166. Judson, David, 413

K

165. Kalb, John, Baron de, 10
165. Kean, John, 174, 228

167. Keeler, Isaac, 42
167. Keeler, Thaddeus, 76
lc. Keese, John, 224
lc. Keith, Israel, 38
lc. Kieth, James, 185
167. Kellar, Adam, 263
165. Kemper, Daniel, 105
165. Kennedy, Samuel, 189, 255
167. Kennedy, Samuel, 302
168. Kennon, John, 442
167. Kersey, William, 1
lc. Kilty, John, Junr., 322
168. Kimmel, Michael, 508
lc. King, Joseph, 254
165. King, Joshua, 133, 251
168. King, Miles, 602
lc. King (or Ring), Richard, 233
166. King, Zebulon, 510
167. Kinney, Samuel, 210
168. Kinnon, John, 467
168. Kinnon, Richard, 371
166. Kirkpatrick, David, 362
165. Kittera, Josiah, 204, 265
166. Knight, Jonathan, 388
167. Knox, George, 274
lc. Knox, Henry, 65
166. Knox, James, 369
167. Knox, William, 264
lc. Kunze, John Christopher, 335

L

167. Lacy, Josiah, 78
165. Lafayette, Marquis de, 9
lc. Lagrace, see Castaing
lc. Lamb, Alexander, 204
166. Lamb, James, 311, 312
lc. Lamb, John, 217
168. Lamb, Nathan, 394
165. Lamb, Thomas, 59
166. Lane, Daniel, 315, 320
167. Lang, James, 269
lc. Langdon, John, 53, 108
166. Lapsley, John, 383
lc. Latimer, Henry, 27
165. Latour, Conrad, 90
165. Laurens, John, 28
165. Lawrence, John, 45
lc. Lawrence, John, 316
166. Lawrence, Jonathan, 365
lc. Lawrence, Joshua, 177
168. Lawson, Claiborne W., 544
lc. Leacraft, George, 210
lc. Learned, Ebenezer, 109
167. Ledlie, Andrew, 228
lc. Lee, Arthur, 345

lc. Lee, Charles, 264
165. Lee, Charles, 2
166. Lee, Daniel, 339
167. Lee, Ezra, 82
168. Lee, John, 424
166. Lesuer, John, 524
165. Leveret, William, 65
168. Lewis, Andrew, 391
165. Lewis, Edward, 160, 250
168. Lewis, William, 597
166. Libby, Jonathan, 499
lc. Lillie, John, 97
165. Lillie, John, 187, 266
167. Little, Andrew, 221
166. Littlefield, John, 447
lc. Lincoln, Benjamin, 298
165. Lincoln, Benjamin, 8
167. Lincoln, Thomas, 219
lc. Lithgow, William, 91
168. Litzsinger, William, 614
165. Livingston, Henry P., 33
lc. Livingston, Robert R., 290
lc. Livingston, Walter, 331
166. Long, Gabriel, 370
166. Long, Reuben, 377
168. Long, William, 583
166. Loomis, Lebbens, 392
167. Lord, James, 83
167. Loree, Ephriam, 6
lc. Loring, Daniel, 110
166. Loring, Jonathan, 316
lc. Loring, Seth, 39
lc. Lovell, Ebenezer, 136
lc. Lovell, James, 135
166. Lovely, William Lewis, 384
lc. Lowden, William, 166
lc. Lowell, John, 320
167. Lowry, John, 189
166. Lunt, Daniel, 466
lc. Lunt, Ezra, 66
166. Lunt, James, 325
167. Lusk, William, 310
lc. Lyman, Daniel, 130
167. Lyon, Abraham, 28
168. Lyon, Benjamin, 327
165. Lyon, Charles, Jr., 155, 215

Mc

168. McAdam, John, 379
167. McBride, Robert, 276
lc. McCall, James, 270, 304
167. McCalla, Mathew, 183
166. McCalla, Thomas Harrison, 569
165. McCaraher, Alexander, 161, 211
165. McCarkey, Alexander, 162

INDEX

McCarter, see Carter
165. McCashlin, James, 197, 273
165. McCaskey, Alexander, 210
165. McClaran, Hugh, 205, 281
167. McClellan, Joseph, 277
167. McClure, William, 167
lc. McConnell, Mathew, 280
168. McCormick, Henry, 334
168. McCowan, John, 344
167. McCracken, William, 208
167. McCullam, John, 314
168. McCully, George, 486
lc. McDonald, Robert, 28
lc. McDougal, Ronald S., 188
168. McDowell, William, 322
168. McElheany, John, 577
168. McFarland, James, 337
167. McGibbony, Patrick, 142
165. McHenry, James, 27
165. McIntosh, Lachlan, 11
167. McIntosh, Lachlan, Jr., 131
167. McKee, Griffith John, 163
166. McKendry, William, 318
166. McKenney, William, 514
McKinley, see Makinly
168. McKinley, John, 383
167. McKinney, John, 281
lc. McKinsily, Samuel, 67
165. McKnight, David, 152, 237
lc. McLane, Daniel, 68
167. McLean, James, 266
167. McMichael, James, 205
167. McMordie, Robert, 243
168. McMurray, William, 474
168. McPherson, Farquher, 355
167. McPherson, Robert, 306

M

166. Maag (Magg), Henry, 546
168. Mabon, James, 459
168. Machenheimer, John, 590
166. Mack (Meek), Alexander, 406
167. Mackey, James, 238
168. Macknet, Charles, 346
167. Magaw, William, 270
Magg, see Maag
167. Makinly (McKinley), Henry, 225
165. Manake (Minka), Christian, 92
166. Manifold, Peter, 564
lc. Manne, Anthony, 172
166. Manson, Theophilus, 435
168. Markland, John, 258
168. Marks, John, 547
165. Marsh, Reuben, 104
166. Marshall, Christopher, 458

168. Marshall, David, 340
168. Marshall, John, 483
165. Marshall, Thomas, 192
165. Marshall, William, 118
167. Martin, Absm., 19
166. Martin, Alexander, 371
167. Martin, Ephriam, 25
lc. Mason, David, 150
168. Massie, Thomas, 464
165. Matthews, Aaron, 112, 199
166. Mattocks, Samuel, 434
168. Maury, Abraham, Jr., 555
lc. Mavings, George, 227
166. Maxwell, Anthony, 357
165. Maxwell, William, 13
166. May, William, 313
166. Mayberry, Richard, 495
Mayers, see Myers
166. Maynard, Jno., 334
166. Maynard, Jonathan, 303
Meek, see Mack
166. Meacham, Jno., 337
167. Mead, Jasper, 62
167. Mead, Matthew, 79
165. Meade, Richard K., 26
166. Means, James, 484
lc. Measam, George, 268
167. Mebane, Robert, 155
166. Meeker, Uzal, 536
lc. Melcher, Isaac, 29
lc. Mellish, Samuel, 45
167. Mentges, Francis, 242
lc. Mercier, John D., 302
166. Merrill, Daniel, 475
168. Meriwether, David, 556
168. Merriwether, James, 419
168. Merriwether, Thomas, 431
168. Mennis, Holman, 600
167. Miel, Charles, 52
168. Miller, David, 369
166. Miller, Henry, 560
167. Miller, Henry, 108
166. Miller, Lemuel, 497
167. Miller, Nicholas, 224
167. Milligan, James, 300
lc. Milligan, James, 13, 263, 294
167. Mills, John, 115
lc. Mills, William, 93
168. Minnis, Callohill, 524
168. Minnis, Francis, 538
lc. Minot, Christopher, 232
167. Mitchell, Alexander, 24
165. Mitchell, John, 126, 175
166. Mitchell, Uriah, 404
168. Mocksley, Rhodam, 438

166. Monell, James, 364
165. Monroe, James, 88
167. Montgomery, Sam., 312
168. Moody, James, 447
168. Moon, Jacob, 568
167. Moore, Isaac, 185
168. Moore, James, 339
166. Moore, Nicholas Ruxton, 579
168. Moore, Thomas, 389
168. Moore, Thomas L., 487
167. Moore, William, 209
165. Morgan, Abel, 125
166. Morgan, Daniel, 368
166. Morgan, David, 544
168. Morgan, Enoch, 357
167. Morgan, Mordecai, 291
168. Morris, Abel, 472
lc. Morris, Gouverneur, 286, 287
lc. Morris, Lewis R., 296
168. Morris, Nathaniel G., 365
lc. Morris, Robert, 283, 284
165. Morris, Samuel, 120, 257
lc. Morse, Charles, 258
165. Morton, George, 156, 218
lc. Mott, Gershom, 203
167. Mott, John, 5
168. Mountjoy, John, 409
166. Moylan, Stephen, 584
165. Muhlenberg, Peter, 20
166. Mulloy, Hugh, 507
167. Murfree (Murphy), Hardy, 151
Murphy, see Murfree
167. Murray, John, 196
lc. Muzzy, Robert, 144
165. Myers (Mayers), Lawrence, 91

N

167. Nagel, George, 248
166. Nason, Joshua, 489, 491
168. Neale, James, 385
166. Neely (Neily), Abraham, 366
167. Neilly, Benjamin, 297
lc. Nelson, George, 31½
lc. Newell (Newhall), Ezra, 160
lc. Newman, Samuel, 83
167. Nice, John, 203
168. Nicholas, John, 430
167. Nichols, Francis, 280
lc. Nichols, Isaac, 192
165. Nicola, Lewis, 80
167. Niker, John B., 17
167. Ninier, James, 119
165. Nitche, John, 110
166. Nivon, (Nivans), Daniel, 350
166. Nixon, Andrew, 572

lc. Nixon, John, 186
lc. Nixon, Thomas, 190
168. Norcross, Aaron, 325
168. North, George, 515
167. North, Caleb, 244
165. North, William, 75
168. Norton, Thomas, 618
168. Norvell, Lipscomb, 368
lc. Nourse, Joseph, 19, 289

O

Oakey, see Okie,
166. Ogden, Barne, 540
166. Ogden, Nathaniel, 534
lc. Okie, Abraham, 325
lc. Oldenbruch, Daniel, 24
168. Oliver, Drury, 563
166. Oliver, Richard, 353
166. Oliver, Robert, 343
166. Olney, Jeremiah, 441
lc. Ord, John, 20
lc. Orr, Alexander, 124
166. Orr, John, 535
lc. Osgood, Samuel, 346, 347
165. Otis, James, 56
165. Otto, Bodo, 188
166. Otto, Bodo, 288
165. Otto, Frederick, 128
168. Overton, John, 551
168. Overton, Thomas, 592
167. Owen, Stephen, 164

P

lc. Paca, William, 266
166. Page, Samuel, 501
lc. Painter, Elisha, 69
165. Palfrey, William, 39
167. Palmer, Edward, 60
168. Parker, Alexander, 443
lc. Parker, Edward, 254
lc. Parker, Joseph, 254
166. Parker, Levi, 326
lc. Parker, Peter, 254
168. Parker, Richard, 533
167. Parker, Samuel F., 21
lc. Parker, Samuel, 254
lc. Parker, Stephen, 70
168. Parker, Thomas, 434
167. Parks, John, 211
166. Parr, James, 385
168. Parramore, Thomas, 587
166. Parsons, David, 593
lc. Parsons, Eli, 161
166. Parsons, Josiah, 446
166. Parsons, Nathan, 455

INDEX

lc. Parsons, Samuel Holden, 351	lc. Porter, Ashbill, 228
168. Paschke, Frederick, 620	166. Porter, Billy, 502
167. Pasteur, Thomas, 174	lc. Porter, Moses, 192
166. Patrick, William, 327	168. Porter, William, 440
167. Patten, John, 173	165. Porterfield, Charles, 101, 130
167. Patterson, John, 106	165. Pool, John, 166, 230
165. Patterson, John, 17	165. Poor, Enoch, 15
167. Patterson, Thomas, 8	166. Pownall, Jno., 300
167. Patton, Robert, 250	166. Prall, Edward, 557
166. Pawling, Albert, 590	166. Pray, John, 492
165. Paxton, James, 81	168. Pride, William, 362
168. Payne, Tarlton, 601	lc. Primer, Matthias, 25
166. Peabody, Ebenezer, 293	166. Prior, Abner, 595
166. Peacock, Hugh, 355	166. Pritch, Thomas, 347
167. Peck, Darius, 92	168. Pugh, Jonathan, 504
167. Peeples, Robert, 313	168. Pursell, Henry D., 617
168. Pelham, Charles, 536	lc. Putnam, Francis, 139
lc. Pell, Philip, 198	
lc. Pemberton, Robert, 337	Q
168. Pemberton, Thomas, 526	lc. Quackenbos, Nicholas, 207
165. Percival, Paul, 141, 242	168. Quarles, Thomas, 451, 459½
167. Perkins, Ebenezer, 94	
lc. Perkins, William, 138	R
167. Perry, Benjamin, 104	lc. Radière, Louis de la, 221
lc. Peters, Richard, 21	165. Ramsay, Thomas, 173, 221
lc. Peters, Thomas, 14	lc. Ramsey, William, 292
lc. Pettingill, Joseph, 176	165. Rand, Abraham, 209, 274
lc. Pettit, Adam, 254	lc. Randall, Thomas, 71
lc. Pettit, Charles, 274, 275	168. Randolph, Edward F., 501
165. Pettit, Charles, 96, 136	165. Ranney (Rooney, Rowney), James, 200
165. Phelon, Edward, 55	
166. Phelps, Seth, 400	lc. Read, George, 318
lc. Phile, Frederick, 32	167. Read, James, 125
165. Philips, David, 181, 208	167. Reading, John, 12
165. Philips, Simon, 157, 217	166. Redding, Zebedee, 527
lc. Pickering, Timothy, 22, 271, 272	167. Reed, Enoch, 90
lc. Pierce, John, 199, 281	168. Reid, Nathan, 572
166. Pierce, Timothy, 416	167. Reily, John, 226
168. Piercy, Henry, 471	166. Remick, Timothy, 479
lc. Pierson, Joseph, 223	lc. Remsen, Charles D., 324
lc. Pike, Benjamin, 196	lc. Remsen, Henry, Jr., 282, 321
166. Pike, Samuel, 302	167. Rice, John, 146
166. Pike, Zebulon, 562	165. Rice, Nathan, 40
lc. Pintard, John, 334	166. Rice, (Royce) Nehemiah, 420
lc. Pinto, Isaac, 344	168. Rice, William, 607
168. Piper, John, 415	167. Richards, William, 95
166. Pixley, Asa, 444	166. Richardson, Abijah, 317
lc. Platt, Richard, 188	lc. Richardson, James, 94
167. Platt, Samuel, 271	167. Richardson, John, 191
166. Plunkett, David, 578	lc. Richie, Robert, 2
168. Pointer, William, 546	lc. Rickman, William, 229
lc. Pollard, Jonathan, 40	165. Riddle, Robert, 283
Ponceau, see Du Ponceau	lc. Ridgwa, Noah, 254
lc. Popkins, John, 125	lc. Riger, see Roger
Portail, see Du Portail	lc. Ring, (or King), Richard, 233

lc. Ripley, Hez'h, 116
165. Risberg, Gustavus, 150, 222
lc. Roane, Spencer, 309
167. Robb, John, 200
166. Robert, John, 588
167. Roberts, John, 145
168. Roberts, John, 456
168. Roberts, Syrus (Cyrus ?) L., 564
168. Robertson, John, 400
167. Robertson, Peter, 112
165. Rodgers, John B., 177
168. Roger (Riger), Anthony, 386
167. Rogers, Hezekiah, 56
165. Rogers, Samuel, 61
168. Roney, John, 375
168. Rose, Alexander, 520
167. Rose, John, 311
166. Rose, Robert, 568
lc. Rosecrans, James, 211
lc. Rouerie, see Armand
165. Rowney (Roney), James, 259
     Royce, see Rice
168. Rudder, Epaphroditus, 421
lc. Ruddock, John, 239
lc. Rush, Jacob, 5
167. Russell, Alexander, 315
168. Russell, Andrew, 372
168. Russell, Charles, 532
167. Russell, Cornelius, 66
168. Ryan, Michael, 329

S

165. Sadler, Matthias, 147, 231
lc. Sale, John, 145
166. Sampson, Crocker, 522
166. Sandford, John, 361
166. Sandford, Samuel, 432
168. Sandridge, Austin, 463
165. Sapel, John Alexander, 146, 234
lc. Sargent, Winthrop, 353
lc. Sarjant, Samuel, 128
168. Saunders, Robert H., 594
166. Savage, Joseph, 592
166. Savage, Henry, 338
168. Savidge, John, 351
165. Scammell, Alexander, 31
lc. Schank, Henry, 184
lc. Schenck, Peter A., 205
168. Schofield, William, 517
167. Schrack, David, 255
166. Schwartz, Godfried, 541
165. Scott, Charles, 21
165. Scott, John, 148, 236
168. Scott, Joseph, 535
lc. Scott, William, 146

167. Scull, John, 132
lc. Scull, Joseph, 95
lc. Sears, Stephen, 222
165. Selden, Charles, 60
167. Selden, Ezra, 88
168. Selden, Joseph, 530
168. Selden, Samuel, 543
165. Selm, Antoin (Selim, Anthony), 93
166. Sewell, Henry, 498
167. Sharp, Anthony, 126
166. Shaw, Benjamin, 516
lc. Shaw, Francis, 209
lc. Shaw, Samuel, 111, 339
167. Sheppard, Abraham, 158
167. Sheppard, John, 153
167. Sheppard, William, 148
167. Sherman, Isaac, 121
166. Shethar, John, 586
168. Shetton, Clough, 411
167. Shipman, Benoni, 111
167. Shippard, (Shepherd), Samuel, 13
lc. Shippen, William, Jr., 15
166. Shrawder, Philip, 556
166. Shrupp, Henry, 553
166. Shugart, Martin, 558
167. Shumway, John, 93
165. Shute, John, 123, 267
167. Shute, Thomas, 190
168. Simms, Charles, 455
lc. Simmons, William, 297
168. Simpson, Michael, 335
165. Skidmore, John J., 114
166. Skidmore, John J., 287
168. Skinner, Alexander, 541
166. Skinner, Elisha, 454
167. Slade, Stephen, 129
167. Slade, William, 128
165. Smallwood, William, 14
lc. Smart, Thomas, 54
168. Smith, Ballard, 539
lc. Smith, Belcher P., 3
lc. Smith, Calvin, 190
166. Smith, David, 431
lc. Smith, Ebenezer, 276
168. Smith, Gregory, 582
167. Smith, Jabez, 57, 64
165. Smith, James, 165, 229
166. Smith, Jno., 335
167. Smith, Job, 75
165. Smith, John, 57
166. Smith, Josiah, 469
168. Smith, Peter, 481
lc. Smith, Resolve, 250
168. Smith, Samuel, 511
168. Smith, William Stirling, 454

INDEX 91

165. Smith, William S., 78
165. Smith, William W., 183
lc. Smock, Robert, 315
168. Snider, Jacob, 468
168. Snider, Philip, 349
166. Snow, Jabez, 298
lc. Soper, Amasa, 84
lc. Souder, Charles, 34
166. Spalding, Simon, 412
167. Speer, Edward, 214
167. Spencer, Ichabod, 89
168. Spencer, John, 559
166. Spencer, Oliver, 539
168. Spiller, Benj. C., 449
168. Springer, Uriah, 382
lc. Square, Jonathan, 242
lc. Stachan, William, 210
lc. St. Clair, Arthur, 348
165. St. Clair, Arthur, 7
168. Staddle, Christian, 470
165. Stagg, John, 94
lc. Stagg, John, Junr., 340
167. Stake, Jacob, 256
166. Stanton, William, 561
167. Starr, Josiah, 49
166. Stebbins, Francis, 304, 336
165. Steel, Archibald, 102, 232
168. Steel, David, 387
168. Steel, John, 361
167. Steel, John, 267
166. Stephens, Ebenezer, 486
165. Steuben, Baron de, 12
167. Stevens, Aaron, 55
lc. Stevens, Amos, 230
lc. Stevens, William, 126
166. Stevens, William, 378
167. Stevenson, Silas, 187
167. Stewart, Charles, 133, 110
lc. Stewart, James, 217
167. Stewart, Walter, 198
165. Stirling, William Alexander, Earl of, 6
167. St. John, John, 77
167. Stokes, John, 462
lc. Stone, Walter, 317
166. Storer, Ebenezer, 487
lc. Story, John, 141
lc. Story, William, 98
167. Stout, Harman, 262
167. Stout, Wessel T., 31
167. Stow, Lazarus, 240
168. Stoy, John, 476
168. Strickler, John, 612
166. Strong, John, 391
167. Strong, Solomon, 71

168. Stubblefield, Veverly, 521
168. Stubblefield, Peter, 429
165. Sullivan, Samuel H., 79
168. Summers, Peter, 506
168. Summers, Simon, 458
166. Sumner, Job, 296
166. Sumner, John, 440
168. Sutton, John, 545
lc. Swaine, John, 328
166. Swan, John, 585
165. Sweeney, Bernard, 143, 241
lc. Sweers, Cornelius, 30
167. Swift, Heman, 58
167. Swyler, Thomas, 287
lc. Symmes, John Cleve, 349

T

168. Talbot, Jeremiah, 350
166. Taliaferro, Benjamin, 374
167. Tanner, Tryal, 37
167. Tarrant, Manlove, 140
167. Tartanson, Francis, 138
168. Tate, James, 484
167. Tate, John, 289
166. Taulman, (Tallman), Peter, 358
167. Taylor, Augustine, 39
lc. Taylor, George, Junr., 330
166. Taylor, Othneil, 448
167. Taylor, Philip, 165
168. Taylor, Richard, 522
lc. Tein, Daniel, 244
166. Temple, Benjamin, 587
166. Ten Eyck, Henry, 120
165. Tennent, Gilbert, 178
166. Tenny, Samuel, 387
165. Ternant, John, 43
167. Terrill, William, 169
168. Terry, Nathaniel, 557
lc. Tetard, John Peter, 307
166. Tew, William, 429
165. Thacher, Nathaniel, 54
lc. Thaxter, John, Jr., 6, 23
166. Thayer, Simeon, 438
165. Thomas, Abishai, 186, 258
167. Thomas, Edmund Disney, 11
lc. Thomas, John, 117
lc. Thomas, Joseph, 118
168. Thomas, Lewis, 390
166. Thomas, Philip, 457
lc. Thompson, Thaddeus, 194
167. Thompson, William, 285
166. Thorp, Eliphalet, 328
167. Tiffany, John, 85
165. Tighlman, Tench, 24
166. Tillinghast, Daniel C., 398

165. Tillotson, Thomas, 47
166. Tisdale, James, 346
168. Tolbert, Samuel, 616
167. Tolly, Mayberry, 241
166. Tom, Nathaniel, 363
lc. Toogood, William, 191
167. Topham, Daniel, 220
167. Torrans, Joseph, 309
lc. Townsend, David, 73
lc. Townsend, James, 206
167. Tracy, Hezekiah, 80
165. Trant, Lawrence, 170, 225
lc. Treadwell, William, 169
165. Trescott, Lemuel, 68
168. Triplett, George, 428
166. Trowbridge, Luther, 307
166. Tubbs, Samuel, 521
166. Tucker, Joseph, 309
168. Tucker, William, 553
168. Tuly, Isaac, 507
166. Tupper, Benjamin, 460
lc. Turnbull, William, 55
lc. Turner, George, 311
167. Turner, Isaac, 114
166. Turner, Jonathan, 443
166. Turner, Peleg, 472
165. Turner, Thomas, 69
lc. Turner, Thomas, 147
166. Tuthill, Samuel, 333
lc. Tyler, Dudley, 197
165. Tyler, John S., 76

U

Upham, Benjamin Allen, 140

V

168. Valentine, Jacob, 531
lc. Vandenburgh, Henry I., 216
167. Vanderslice, Jacob, 273
168. Vanderwall, Marks, 542
lc. Van Hook, Arondt, 240
165. Van Harn, David, 67
167. Vanlear, William, 279
167. Varner, Robert, 123
165. Varnum, James Mitchell, 16
lc. Varnum, James Mitchell, 352
168. Vaughn, Claiborne, 595
167. Vaughn, George, 233
lc. Velie, Cornelius, 245
167. Vernon, Frederick, 293
168. Vernon, Job, 518
166. Viol, John, 390
165. Voorhies, Minne, 168, 227

W

166. Wadsworth, Joseph, 520
167. Wadsworth, Roger, 70
166. Wait, Daniel, 394
167. Walbridge, Ames, 117
166. Wale(s), Jacob, 442
165. Walker, Benjamin, 42
lc. Walker, Benjamin, 329
168. Walker, David, 566
168. Walker, Levin, 584
165. Walker, Richard, 63
lc. Wallcutt, Benjamin, 85
166. Wallen, Jonathan, 436
167. Walton, William, 170
168. Waples, Samuel, 589
165. Ward, Joseph, 86
166. Warner, William, 453
166. Warren, Benjamin, 305
lc. Warren, John, 74
165. Washington, George, 1
166. Washington, William, 580
166. Watkins, Nathan, 476
lc. Watson, Abraham, 133
167. Watson, Titus, 46
166. Watts, David, 488
166. Watts, John, 573
168. Waugh, James, 348
165. Wayne, Anthony, 18
166. Weatherby, Benjamin, 530
167. Weaver, Jacob, 218
166. Weeks, Nathan, 417
lc. Weeks, Thomas, 208
165. Weems, James, 51
168. Weidman, John, 610
168. Welch, Nathaniel, 448
165. Welsh, Enoch, 38
166. Weltner, Ludwick, 555
lc. Wesson, James, 119
166. West, Ebenezer, 407
168. West, Thomas, 408
167. Weymon, Abel, 26
lc. Wheeler, Adam, 189
lc. Wheeler, Nathan, 189
166. Wheelwright, Daniel, 496
166. White, Anthony W., 583
166. White, George, 500
lc. White, James, 342
lc. White, John, 31, 241
166. White, John, 115
167. White, Nicholas, 239
166. White, William, 323
165. Whitehead, James, 117, 164
166. Whiting, Daniel, 314
165. Whiting, Timothy, 179, 213

Index

167. Whitlock, Ephm., 20
165. Whittelsey, Charles, 35, 254
lc. Whitwell, Samuel, 86
lc. Wiggans, Thomas, 319
168. Wigton, John, 485
167. Wilcox, Jas., (or Joe), 54
lc. Wild, Samuel, 162
165. Wiley, Thomas, 144, 244
167. Wilkinson, Nathan, 7
165. Wilkinson, Nathan, 121, 256
165. Willett, Marinus, 124
lc. Willetts, Caja, 254
166. Williams, Abraham, 482
167. Williams, Benjamin, 147
168. Williams, James, 401
166. Williams, Jos., 295
lc. Williams, Robert, 75
168. Williams, William, 475
167. Williamson, James, 307
165. Williamson, James, 277, 278
166. Williamson, Samuel, 570
167. Willson, James, 186
165. Wilson, Goodwin, 190
168. Wilson, James, 331
166. Wingate, John, 481
lc. Winn, Richard, 350

166. Winslow, Nathaniel, 463
lc. Winston, John, 76
168. Wirtenberg, Lodowick, 608
168. Woelper, John D., 598
167. Womack, William, 161
168. Wood, Abraham, 514
166. Wood, Daniel, 359
167. Woodbridge, Theodore, 40
165. Woodford, William, 19
167. Woodruff, Aaron, 223
lc. Woodruff, Aaron D., 260
168. Woodson, Frederick, 432
168. Worsham, John, 585
168. Worsham, Richard, 549
167. Wright, David, 192
lc. Wright, Edward, Jr., 310
167. Wright, Joseph Allyn, 61

Y

166. Yancy, Robert, 563
168. Yarborough, Charles, 529
166. Young, Marcus, 542
165. Yule, James, 196, 280

Z

168. Ziegler, David, 328

www.ingramcontent.com/pod-product-compliance
Lightning Source LLC
Chambersburg PA
CBHW071626170426
43195CB00038B/2149